Miraculous Encounters

Miraculous Encounters

True Stories of Experiences
with
Angels and Departed Loved Ones

Michele A. Livingston

authorHOUSE™

1663 LIBERTY DRIVE, SUITE 200
BLOOMINGTON, INDIANA 47403
(800) 839-8640
WWW.AUTHORHOUSE.COM

First published by AuthorHouse 07/22/05

ISBN: 1-4184-8808-9 (e)
ISBN: 1-4184-8809-7 (sc)
ISBN: 1-4184-8810-0 (dj)

Library of Congress Control Number: 2004095771

Printed in the United States of America
Bloomington, Indiana

This book is printed on acid-free paper.

Cover design by Jon R. Stroh

Cover Picture "The Descent of the Holy Spirit" painted by Michele A. Livingston for her
book Visions from Mary, 1999, Blue Mantle Press.

Edited by Gayle Crist and Jon Stroh

Back cover and book jacket text by Fred Lauver

Other books by Michele A. Livingston

Visions from Mary

Echoes in the Wind: Messages from the Tribes of the
Nation
Volume 1, The Lakota (Sioux) Nation

Messages from Beyond the Veil: A Selection of "Group
Information" from the Sessions of Michele A. Livingston

Available from author at <u>Michele@michelelivingston.com</u> or
phone 717.737.3888

To
Angels and Departed Loved Ones
Everywhere

Acknowledgements

I wish to first thank all the individuals who sincerely and lovingly submitted their true stories for publication. All have touched my heart.

Next, I acknowledge and thank my husband and soul partner, Jon Robert Stroh for his dedication and support during this project.

With gratitude I thank my editors Gayle Crist and Jon Stroh.

Finally I acknowledge Fred Lauver for composing the cover and book jacket text.

Contents

    An Angel from the Mercy Band
    Evan's Angels by Karen H.
    Pushed to Safety by Regina H.
    It's Not Your Time by Lilly T.
    Michael's Healing Prayers by C. J. C.
    Celestial Beings by Kathy B.
    The Shoe Store Angels by Susan Z.
    Divine Intervention by Charlotte M.
    Stranger in a Leather Jacket by Becca T.
    God's Divine Force by Lynn M.
    Guiding Grandma Home by Beth H.
    Angela's Butterfly Angel by Mark P.
    Saved by an Angel by Sandi A.
    A Higher Power by Debbi S.
    My Angel of Light by Catherine G.
    Rydell's Healing Presence by Ray W.
    Just in Time by Maureen F.
    Miraculous Intervention by Debra C.
    Thanks, Nancy by Dawn C.
    Angelic Occurrences by Ellen B.
    Comments from Michele
    A Piece of Heaven by Ruth C.
    The Rooftop Angels by Ruth C.

Part II: Departed Loved Ones

*"There are two ways to live your life.
One is as though nothing is a miracle.
The other is as though everything is."*
– Albert Einstein

Preface

My Journey

*"A **miracle** is a gift of unconditional love that can transform those who doubt, change people in positive ways, and teach them that God, the Creator, is ever constant, faithful, and present with us." – Michele Livingston*

My story begins before I took my first breath—the "breath of life." The first thing I remember is hovering, somehow, on the ceiling of the delivery room. It was 1951. The room was tiled in green with very bright lights. I heard a voice say, "It's time to go down." But, I didn't want to go down, so I remained floating on the ceiling. Suddenly, it felt like I was on a chute or a sliding board, and hands were pushing me down. That was the moment I entered my body!

After that, I have little memory until I was about 2 years old. I had the *spiritual amnesia* all babies have when their *old soul* enters a new baby's body. It was interesting that, when I was old enough to understand, my mother Dorothy told me about her *vision*. It was something I would never forget.

One night, during the fifth month of her pregnancy, my mother saw me in a very lucid dream! I was a little dark-haired child, out in infinite space, looking at the world with all the twinkling stars around it—and I was shaking my head "NO!" I really didn't want to come to the earth-plane at that time. But I was on a mission, though it took me years to discover exactly what the mission was.

My mother was in her mid-40s and had just married my dad, Lear, who was 50. She had prayed for a little girl, but the doctors told her not to get her hopes up. They had discovered a fibroid tumor the size of a grapefruit in her uterus and told her she had to have a hysterectomy when she returned from her honeymoon. Shortly after she returned, she went in for a presurgery examination and … they discovered she was *pregnant* with ME! And that was not the only miracle—I actually grew right around the tumor!

I was born with a clubfoot, which my mother faithfully massaged daily to prevent me from having to wear leg braces. But for the first several years, my soul was still trying to decide if it should stay in this new body or go back to the beautiful heavenly realms of love and light; therefore, I almost died several times during my early childhood.

One of these incidents occurred before we even left the hospital! Because of Dorothy's precarious medical condition, they kept her hospitalized with me the first two weeks of my life. One morning, around 2 a.m., my mother sat straight up in bed and screamed, "My baby is dying!" She got out of bed and ran down the hall in bare feet towards the nursery section of the hospital. Two nurses tried to restrain her, but she insisted on seeing me. Weighing only five pounds, I had just missed the incubator and was in the main nursery section. When the nurse came to my crib, she found I had turned blue and was not breathing.

Phlegm had collected in my throat—I was literally choking to death! They got to me just in time to save my life. This incident, when I was only 3 days old, developed a never-ending *soul bond* between Dorothy and me. Of course, my dad, at age 50, was thrilled with his new miracle child—his only child. Then, at age two, I looked at my mother and said, "Mama, I'm glad I picked you to be my mama!" I'd tell her that often. When she held me, she said she knew I was an *old soul*—she could see it in my eyes.

So, what was the mission I was sent down to accomplish? I feel it's the work I do today. I bridge the gap between dimensions for other people. I am the liaison between the earth-plane and the world of spirit. I have seen many *miracles* and have experienced in my 53 years of life things that other people can only imagine. I have seen and communed with my own angels, spirit guides, and loved ones on the other side, and I have brought others closer to theirs.

This didn't happen overnight. Discovering my mission was an evolutionary process of self-awareness. My first 38 years on Earth were spent as an artist and teacher. I started drawing and painting at the age of three and had my first "one-man show" in the sixth grade. I graduated with a Master's degree from Penn State University and taught art in the inner city for 10 years. I then left and developed an art business, and I traveled the country participating in art shows.

This business led me into opening my own art gallery, where I displayed all the prints, paintings, and porcelain collector's plates I had designed over many years. This "Part One" of my life was dedicated to enlightening others and bringing them joy through my artwork.

Today, when I do television and radio interviews, the first question usually is: "When did you know you had this gift for being a visionary?" And my answer is: "I was at an art show selling a piece of my work to a stranger, and I saw the initials "L.R." floating above the lady's head. I wondered what in the world they were doing there. When I asked her name, it happened to be Laura Roberts—which correlated with the L.R. This surprised me at the time, but that incident became the beginning of my new career." Next, an interviewer usually asks me how I started seeing human souls from the spirit world. And my answer is, "It simply happened!"

I was participating in a metaphysical conference at my alma mater, and in front of me sat a lady who wanted to receive *impressions* from me about her life. I looked up at her, and there was a man—a human soul—standing beside her, on my left. I could *see* him plainly. He wore a light blue shirt, his hairline was receding, and he had a pleasant demeanor. He was also translucent—I could see right through him!

I wasn't at all afraid, just rather shocked. I thought to myself, "I wonder why he's standing next to her?" At that moment, he telepathically sent back this message, "My name is John, and I'm her grandfather!" I timidly asked her, "Do you happen to have a grandfather named John?" The lady looked surprised and slowly answered, "Yes ... why are you asking me that?" I said, "He's standing right next to you." She said, "What does he want?" I telepathically asked him, and he held up four fingers. I asked her if four meant anything to her, and she said, "Why, yes. I have four daughters." (I have since learned fingers always represent the number of people the soul wants to acknowledge.)

With that, the spirit of John nodded in agreement and proceeded to give me information about each one of his granddaughters. He described how he protects them and is especially fond of the one named after her mother. The lady's mouth dropped open—she got more than she bargained for that day!

After that first *visionary* experience, I myself wondered why this had occurred so suddenly. As an avid Bible student, I remembered the verse, "As to whom much is given, much is required" (Luke 12:48) and pondered it. I came to the conclusion I was not mature or focused enough before age 38 to handle the responsibility of this gift. Indeed, it is a whole lifestyle readjustment. Extra rest, good nutrition, soaking baths, walks in nature, and prayer and meditation time are *musts*. Fifteen years later, this gift never ceases to amaze me, because I myself need constant reaffirmations and confirmations ...and I always receive them. I continue to do this work to let others know they are not alone.

God is the source of all that is, and our souls are eternal and indestructible. We shed the physical shell or body, like the metamorphosis of the butterfly, and then we fly free once more. The soul retains its memories, its mind, and its personality. It still loves us here on Earth, since love never dies. By making others aware of this, it gives them hope, knowing they will join those they've loved and lost to physical death. I feel my gift is meant to encourage, uplift, and bring hope to others on their journey through the physical world.

Through my travels, I've met people who stop me and say, "Do you want to hear my story?" "Can I share my experience with you?" These constant questions spurred me to think about compiling a book with these compelling stories, and that's how the idea for this book was born! This is a compilation of stories—based on the true experiences I've received from others. They were submitted at my seminars and through e-mails and letters. Some of these individuals have been changed by their experiences, and for others a new spiritual realm has emerged.

These encounters include protection and appearances by angels, communiqués from departed loved ones, and even sightings of spirit messengers from the animal and insect kingdoms. They are woven together with a common thread of truth, sincerity, and unconditional love. In essence, they are miracles that are impossible to explain by means of the laws of nature—they are supernatural events. To me, a *miracle* is a gift of unconditional love that can transform those who doubt, change people in positive ways, and teach them that God, the Creator, is ever constant, faithful, and present with us. But best of all, these *miraculous encounters* remind us that we are *never alone*!

I've included one or more of my own personal experiences at the beginning of most chapters, and now I hope these *miraculous encounters* will amaze and move you as they have me.

Michele A. Livingston

PART I

ANGELS

1

Chapter One

Angelic Encounters

"Make yourself familiar with the angels, and behold them frequently in spirit: for without being seen, they are present with you." – St. Francis de Sales

In many seminars and interviews, I'm asked, "What are angels?" Through extensive experience, reading, prayer, and meditation time, I've come to the following conclusion: angels are *light beings* created by God to travel with us on our journey through eternity. They have never been a human soul but can take on human form in times of need. They don't have free choice and will as human souls do but instead take assignments from the Creator.

There are many kinds and levels of angels. *Guardian angels* never leave our side. They protect, oversee, and inspire our development. *Birthing angels* will bring their energy around a mother who is giving birth, assisting a soul as it enters a new baby's body with the first breath—the *breath of life*. *Project angels* are assigned to us in order to help us with certain endeavors or pursuits—writing a book, painting a picture, composing a song, building a new house, and so on. These angels stay until the project is completed and then leave. Angels act as *coaches* in the game of life.

Transition or *death angels* come for us when we are making our transition from the third to the fourth dimension. *Archangels* oversee certain dimensions and realms and are given more responsibility than regular angels. Archangel Michael is the "Divine Protector"— he protects humans and shields them from negativity and harm. Archangel Gabriel is the "Divine Messenger of Truth." He was directed to deliver *the news* to Mary about the conception of Jesus and *announced* the birth of John the Baptist. Archangel Raphael is the "Divine Healer." He oversees hospitals and those who are ill and heralds into the earth-plane other healing angels. Most archangels and many guardian angels have an "el" in their name. "El" is from Hebrew and means "like unto God" or "coming from God."

There are 12 dimensions of light and energy—the "Angelic Kingdom" is in the 11th dimension. Angels are androgynous (or sexless), and they don't have wings. They emanate a bright light or aura that people sometimes *perceive* as "halos" and "white wings." The following are stories people have sent me, based on their actual experiences with angels, but first I'd like to start the chapter with one of my own.

An Angel from the Mercy Band

My first angelic encounter happened when I was 15. My father had passed away suddenly from a brain tumor, and I was in total shock ...so much so that I started to retreat from reality. My mother recognized the warning signs and tried to bring me out of my shell. She took part of our savings and sent me to Europe for the summer with the Foreign Language League ...an endeavor that started my healing and led me on the road to recovery.

During the trip, I instantly bonded with Sara—a very bright and funny 14-year-old. We rapidly became friends and were so preoccupied with our own interests that, one day, the two of us got lost in Paris. Being unaware of time, we missed our return destination point, becoming detached from the rest of the group. We headed toward the Paris subway and tried to figure out what to do. She spoke better French than I did, so we decided to wait until someone came by that she could ask for directions. But strangely, on that summer afternoon in 1966, there weren't a lot of people in the Paris subway. We felt desperate and started to cry. Finally, we took each other's hands and prayed to God for help.

Suddenly a *mist* literally rolled down the subway, and out of that mist stepped a tall, white-haired gentleman wearing a white suit and a gold badge that said, "International Guide." Sara jumped at the opportunity to speak French to him and pleaded with him for help. But before she could continue, he replied to us in perfect English, "There's no need for French. You see, I'm an International Guide and speak all languages. In fact, I'm on my way to oversee a meeting with President Charles De Gaulle!" He announced, "You girls are lost and need help to get back to Orsay!" We couldn't believe he knew where we were trying to go! The whole event was becoming surreal.

We followed him like little lambs onto the subway car. He proceeded to pay our fare and rode with us to Orsay. On the way, he told us about ourselves. Sara, he exclaimed, was an excellent student. I, on the other hand, needed to apply myself and study more. At the time, we didn't delve into how he knew this information; we just took it at face value. About an hour later, we pulled into the Orsay station, and Sara and I hopped out of the subway car. The white-haired gentleman followed us.

We immediately turned around to thank him once more, but he had vanished. As we looked down the long stretch of subway, a mist rolled through again …and that was it! Sara looked at me and said, "Do you think that was an angel?" In our childlike innocence, we agreed and thought nothing more about it. But it must have been our simple, childlike prayer that brought an angel to the rescue that day!

Needless to say, we were in big trouble with the Foreign Language League. We were drastically reprimanded for being so foolish; but the incident was soon forgotten, and I returned to the United States. However, the memory of that day stayed in the back of my mind.

One night about a year later, I had a lucid dream. I entered a room where there were about 100 people—both male and female—all with white hair and dressed in white. As I milled through the crowd, the same white-haired gentleman who'd *saved* Sara and me in Paris caught my eye from the corner of the room! He wore the same white suit and slowly walked over to me. He stood in front of me—tall, elegant, and smiling—and he simply said, "We are all angels here. We're called the 'Mercy Band' and take human form in times of need. When your prayer was sent to Heaven, I was sent down to help you."

With that, I awoke. "Wow!" I thought. "Angels *do* exist!" How lucky I was at such a tender age to have experienced one. It didn't occur to me at the time that this was just the beginning of a wonderful journey.

Evan's Angels
by Karen H.

My precious 4-year-old son Evan was in his room playing on the day after Easter, 2003. He decided he was going to be Spiderman, and he climbed up on his corner cabinet. Even though the cabinet was quite heavy, when Evan jumped off of it, it fell forward and ended up landing on top of him. I heard him scream, "Mommy!" When I entered his room, his little legs were pinned under the cabinet. He was crying, and blood was streaming from his mouth and nose.

I tried to move the cabinet, but it had fallen on him in an awkward position and was just too heavy to move. I told him I was going to call for help, while I wiped his tears and blood. I ran down the hall to call "911." They told me to remain calm and to keep Evan as calm as possible. We talked on the phone for just a couple of minutes, but it seemed like everything around me was hazy and moving in slow motion. When I returned to Evan's room, I saw something amazing—the cabinet had been moved off of his legs and was lying beside him!

Evan's legs were badly bruised and cut, but, miraculously, it didn't seem like any bones were broken. He was tired, so I didn't question him about how the cabinet had been moved. We went to the hospital, where a battery of tests and X-rays were done. Evan was a little trooper, and the doctors said there were no internal injuries or broken bones. After being in the hospital for two days, our little boy was home with us again.

On the evening Evan came home, I lay down with him to pray before bed, as we always did. I said, "Evan, what do you want to pray for tonight?" Without hesitation, he said, "I want to thank God for coming down from Heaven to pull me out from underneath the cabinet." Well, I think he could tell by my face that I was quite shocked. So I asked him, "What did God look like?" Evan said he had light brown hair, "just like you and me, Mommy," and blue eyes. He was wearing a white robe with "rainbow colors" all around it, and he had wings. "Evan," I said, "that sounds like your guardian angel."

He said there were even little boys and girls in his room who had wings. The boys had white hair, and the girls had brown. They wore blue and white robes. I told him they sounded like "cherubs." I asked Evan if he was scared when the big angel came down to help, and he said, "No, Mommy, because he took my hand and said, 'Don't be afraid; I'm going to pull you out, and it won't hurt.'"

I also asked Evan if the little cherubs said anything, and Evan said, "Yes! They said, 'Ouch! That must've hurt!'" (That was so cute; it made me laugh inside.) Evan also said the big angel "looked like Jesus and flew up through the ceiling." Finally, Evan concluded his story by saying, "I liked the most when my angel pulled me out because the whole room was sparkly and really beautiful."

There's an old saying: "Out of the mouths of babes comes the truth." The purity and sincerity with which Evan told his story convinced me that angels *do* exist. They certainly made a miracle happen for my little boy that day!

Pushed to Safety
by Regina H.

One early fall morning in 1993, my father and I were heading down the interstate with a truckload of furniture. My fiancé and I had bought a new home, and Dad was helping me move the things from my apartment to the new house.

All at once, we heard sputtering and clicking sounds in the truck, and then the power steering locked up. It caught us by surprise, but Dad managed to steer the truck to safety on the shoulder of the road.

It was an eerie feeling to be stranded alone, without a cell phone handy.

Then, out of the blue, a white car pulled up behind us. A man approached who looked like a policeman. At least, he was in a uniform and was very polite. He offered to push us to the next off ramp, where he said there was a gas station. We agreed and let him begin pushing us. However, within seconds, we had drifted across all three lanes and into oncoming traffic.

I closed my eyes and prayed for our safety. Just then, Dad sighed heavily in relief because he had been able to regain control of the truck, and the white car behind us was once again able to push us back into the right lane to safety. Luckily, and unbelievably, there wasn't a lot of traffic that fall morning.

The police officer in the white car continued to push us slowly down the ramp and then safely into the gas station. Dad and I just sat there and looked at each other. What a break! Dad got out of the truck to go back and thank the officer and to get his name and badge number so he could write a letter of commendation to his sergeant. But, when Dad looked behind us, the white car had vanished!

When we asked the people at the station if they saw the car leave, they said they hadn't even seen a white car push us in. It was like the police officer had never existed! We now think the officer was an angel who took human form in our time of need. We know for sure that we were both protected that day when he ultimately pushed us to safety!

It's Not Your Time
by Lilly T.

I'm a 68-year-old waitress who's been serving the public for almost 50 years. I'm the mother of four children and the grandmother of eight. My life has been a simple one, and I've never thought much about angels or other beings. While I've heard stories about other people who've seen angels or who had dreams that have come true, nothing like that had ever happened to me or my family. But all that changed two years ago!

I woke up one night around 2 a.m. with terrible chest pains. My one daughter drove me to the emergency room of our local hospital where I was immediately put into intensive care and given all kinds of tests. I became very weak, and the doctors told me later that I passed out. All I know is that I was floating above my body and looking down at myself thinking, "Why am I up here on the ceiling?"

A blue light filled the emergency room, and I began to float higher and higher. It was so peaceful and quiet. I saw a light that looked like the sun, only brighter. Then, I found myself walking upright and going towards it. Suddenly, a "being" came toward me. I couldn't see its face, but it had a white robe on with a hood over its head. It said very loudly, "It's not your time! Go back!" But I didn't want to go back to Earth, because the light was pulling me in, and it made me feel so calm and happy.

Next, the being raised its hands and gently pushed me backwards. It said again, even more plainly, "Go back. Go back—it's not your time!" Just then, I woke up as if from a trance and saw all my children standing around my bed looking at me. They said I had "flat-lined," and they thought they had lost me. I told my children what I'd seen and experienced, but they didn't believe me. They said I was dreaming …but *I* know different!

I believe now that the being I saw was my angel who came to tell me it wasn't my time to go. I also believe that, when it *is* my time, I won't be afraid. It will be a very peaceful and wonderful experience to cross to the other side.

Michael's Healing Prayers
by C. J. C.

A very good Christian friend of mine is a wife and mother of two children. Over the years, she has had a severe problem with depression and panic attacks. Once, while she was in the hospital and feeling hopeless, she met a young man named Michael behind the counter at the nurse's station, located in the front hall. He was very attractive, with glasses, and wearing what looked like a white lab coat.

As she approached the counter that evening, he stepped out from behind it and asked her if she needed help. Upon hearing that she felt hopeless, he offered to pray with her. At first, she turned down his offer; certain that she didn't need any help. But later, after returning to her room, she reconsidered and decided to walk back down the hall to talk to him. At that very moment, he appeared at her open doorway! So they knelt down and prayed together. Their praying together was a powerful experience that helped her have a very quick recovery—much faster than she'd had in the past. She felt very grateful and wanted to thank the young man for blessing her with his prayers.

So, after she returned home a week later, she called the hospital to try and reach the man. But the hospital said they had no record of a man named Michael who fit that description and worked on that floor. She described him in greater detail, but again they said no one by that name, wearing glasses and a white lab coat, worked on any shift at that location. Eventually, she gave up trying to find him or to figure out who he was.

A couple of months later, I wound up as partners with my friend, alone in a rowboat at a women's retreat we both attended. As we talked and got to know each other better, she shyly shared her story about the mysterious man. I suggested he might be a guardian angel, but that was something she didn't really believe in. However, later that day at lunch, a group of ladies who joined us began telling their angel stories. Suddenly, I saw tears starting to stream down my friend's face. She now realized she was being given a message: guardian angels *do* exist. And that day in the hospital, Michael had been hers!

Celestial Beings
by Kathy B.

I was eight months' pregnant with my first child and driving my car home from a tiring shopping trip. Suddenly, another car pulled out from a used car lot—directly in front of me! When I tried to hit the brakes, the steering wheel literally spun free from my hands, and I heard a very loud noise under my car. It felt like my car was being picked up and jerked into the lane next to mine!

I then grabbed the wheel again, without trying to evaluate what had just happened. But I had an *instant knowledge* that there were two beings beneath my car who were responsible for lifting it and moving it to a safer location. Then, it dawned on me: maybe these were guardian angels—one for me and one for my unborn child!

Upon arriving home, I told my husband what had happened and asked him to crawl under the car to see if he could figure out what had caused the loud noise. He found nothing and had no explanation. To this day, we have no idea what really happened to save my baby and me that day. But *I* know I was headed straight into the side of that other car, and angels or some other celestial beings *saved* us from disaster!

The Shoe Store Angels
by Susan Z.

In the fall of 1990, I was a young woman, working as a social worker by day and moonlighting at a shopping mall shoe store in Pennsylvania by night. We never seemed to have any customers in the evenings; in fact, it was rather desolate and dimly lit. My parents expressed their concerns—that it wasn't very safe, being in the store alone at night and then walking out the back door to my car. Of course, like most independent young adults, I ignored them and continued working there.

One evening around 6 p.m., a dark-haired, unshaven man entered the store. He asked if my manager was there, and I let my guard down and said no. He proceeded to pick up the first pair of shoes he saw and asked to try them on in his size. I walked to the rear of the store, through a counter area, and into the storeroom. There was a sign on the door of the storeroom that said "Employees Only."

Suddenly, the man was directly behind me—he crept up without a sound. He grabbed my arm, pushed me against the wall, and shoved me down towards the floor. I have been able to sense danger since I was a child, and, at that moment, I *knew* I was in great danger. I closed my eyes and silently started to pray, "Oh, please God, help me! Please help me!"

At that moment, the man glanced through the glass door of the storage area into the main store and said, "You have all kinds of customers out there; you better go wait on them first." As I left the storeroom, I was shaking and slowly walked to the register where the phone was. Standing beside the phone was a tall, strikingly handsome man with blue eyes. Our eyes locked, and he calmly said, "It's OK; everything is going to be OK."

As I looked around me, I saw that, in addition to that man, the store was now filled with dozens of customers! Honestly, there must have been at least 50 people walking around me. They seemed to have appeared from nowhere! I was confused and thought the tall man next to the phone may have been the other man's accomplice, but he seemed so reassuring to me that I felt strangely safe when he spoke those words.

The next couple of seconds seemed like hours; and as I was reaching for the phone to call for help, my manager, Bob, appeared at the door. He had forgotten something and, by the grace of God, had returned. I mouthed the words, "Don't leave me!"

Then, as I looked around, the store was empty—as quickly as it had been filled with people, they had all vanished! The tall handsome man standing by the phone was gone too, but the bad guy was still hanging around the store.

Bob knew something was wrong and had the good sense not to leave me. Since the mall now seemed empty, he made the decision to close the store early and told the strange man to leave. I was so shaken, I had Bob walk me to my car. Soon after that, I took my parents' advice and quit that job. I was just too scared to work there alone anymore.

About eight months later, I was sitting at my desk at my daytime job when the phone rang. It was a detective from the Police Department. He needed me to recall some incidents of that particular evening with the strange man in the shoe store. "Do you remember anything from that night and can we talk to you?" he asked. I said I could, so the detective and his assistant came over to my place of employment and had me look at a stack of pictures. From them I was able to identify the man for them. The strange man in question was a known rapist who carried a gun and knife. He had a fetish for young blondes in shoe stores. He was at large and was wanted for numerous counts of rape and assault and battery throughout the northeastern U.S. I was to be his next victim!

I shook and sobbed when they told me that the man next went to a Payless Shoe Store in the area and raped a young employee at knifepoint. They were on his trail, but needed help in prosecuting him. A couple months later, in court, I testified against him.

Then I had an epiphany! The kind, tall man with the beautiful blue eyes at the register was an angel! He had calmed me down, which helped to save my life. The customers filling the store—seeming to come from nowhere—were also angels. They appeared to divert my assailant and then disappeared into thin air!

I am so blessed and eternally grateful to them for hearing my desperate prayer for help. I have always been a believer, but I never dreamt I would meet a heavenly host of angels in a shoe store!

Divine Intervention
by Charlotte M.

When my son Jeffrey was 3½, he was a beautiful, precocious boy, his eyes filled with wonder. He loved animals and always got very excited whenever he saw one. When we took him to a petting zoo, we literally had to watch him every second. He would dart back and forth, wanting to touch and talk to every single animal. It was all we could do to contain him.

One warm July day, Jeffrey and I were taking a walk in our neighborhood. The streets were very quiet, and we were admiring everything. Suddenly, Jeffrey cried, "Look, Mama! A puppy!" There was a small dog tied out on a rope in a neighbor's front yard. My son immediately started to dash across the street to play with the dog.

A split second later, out of nowhere, a car came speeding down the street toward us. I screamed, "Jeffrey! Stop!" He was within inches of the front tire of the speeding car! As I ran toward him, I saw him being lifted into the air by an invisible being! He was thrown backward toward the grass, where he landed safely.

This all happened so fast, I couldn't even see the car's license plate. I was stunned as I examined Jeffrey's body. There wasn't a scratch on him! He nonchalantly said, "Don't worry, Mama. My angel saved me." This incident opened my eyes to the invisible world of angels—a world of love, protection, and miracles.

Stranger in a Leather Jacket
by Becca T.

Last year, when I was 13 and in 7th grade, my mother and I had a very mysterious encounter. My mother is a teacher at the school I attend, though I'm not in her class. She had dismissed her class early one day in late May, because she and I were hurrying to pick up my younger brothers from their school.

As we were leaving, a girl named Jenny fell through a glass door and badly injured her arm. There was blood everywhere, so my mother immediately called an ambulance from her cell phone. Suddenly, a stranger in a black leather jacket appeared at the top of the stairs. My mother didn't see him approach and had no idea where he'd come from. She thought it was odd that she'd never seen him before and that he was wearing a leather jacket, because it was very warm outside.

The stranger walked over to help. He wrapped his jacket tightly around Jenny's arm to stop the bleeding. A few seconds later, he said he had to leave, that he was needed elsewhere, and he disappeared down the stairs. Just then, the medical team came rushing up the stairs to carry Jenny to the ambulance. Her arm was still wrapped tightly in the stranger's jacket. The medics said the tight jacket worked as a tourniquet to stop the bleeding and was the best thing that could have been done for her.

Immediately, my mother ran to look for the man to thank him, but he was nowhere in sight. She asked the medical team if they saw him coming down the steps as they came up. But they said they hadn't seen anyone. To this day, my mother believes that the stranger must have been Joshua (the form of Jesus as a mortal) or Jenny's guardian angel. We'll never know for sure. All that *is* certain is that heavenly help came for Jenny that day.

God's Divine Force
by Lynn M.

Many times while driving in my van with my two young children, I've felt like we were *saved* in very close calls. Each time, I'd be guided to turn the wheel or hit the brake at the last second to avoid an accident. There is one incident, though, that stands out in my mind. I will never forget it.

On this occasion, I was sitting in a shopping center parking lot with both kids, who were in their car seats in the back. I was getting ready to pull out of my space, but something prompted me to sit there for a minute before proceeding. I felt paralyzed, unable to move. A couple of seconds passed and then, suddenly—out of nowhere—a car came speeding through the parking lot right behind us, going at what seemed to me to be at least 70 miles an hour! He was going so fast, his car was no more than a streak of color going by.

After I calmed down, I thought for a moment and realized that, if I hadn't waited those extra few seconds like I did, that car would have wiped out the entire back of my van where my children were—first crushing the side where my baby Rachel was sitting. I was so relieved and grateful that my children and I were safe! Then, I began to feel very strongly that an unknown and unseen power of some kind had saved our lives that day by instantly immobilizing me as I got ready to pull out.

Guiding Grandma Home
by Beth H.

It was the month of August, the Sunday of Labor Day weekend, eight years ago. I had a vision that I will never forget. In my dream, I woke up when I heard the downstairs TV turned on in the den. I became anxious with fear because I thought everyone in the house was upstairs sleeping, just like me. Slowly, I walked downstairs and rounded the corner into the den, with my heart beating like a drum.

I was surprised to see my young daughter sitting on the couch watching TV. The light in the room was abnormally bright, but the layout was the same. Across the room, at the sliding glass patio door, there was a small blonde child kneeling down. The door was open, and the child was bathed in bright light, wearing white, and appeared to have wings.

The room seemed very cool. As I stood in the doorway, my little daughter, still sitting on the couch, looked up at me and said, "It's OK, Mommy, don't be afraid. The angel has come for Grandma!" My heart was still pounding, and I started to cry as my sweet daughter remained calm and smiling.

I woke up from my dream and couldn't believe I was still in bed—the vision had been so real. I mentioned the dream in passing to my family, but I didn't give any details because I honestly thought they wouldn't believe me. Also, I didn't want to deal with the thought of losing my mother.

About three months later, my mother passed away after a long, painful illness. I truly feel the dream was a sign for me and that the angel was my mother's guardian who was coming to take her home. My mother and daughter were very close, and I found it remarkable that in the dream my little girl approached the inevitable in such a calm and loving way.

I recorded my vision in my computer because I didn't want to forget any details. I believe we all have an angel who helps us through life and will be there to gently guide us home.

Angela's Butterfly Angel
by Mark P.

My wife Pat was always into angels. She'd been collecting them for many years by the time we were married. In fact, we named our daughter Angela because of Pat's love for angels. I myself was never much of a believer in angels because the idea didn't make logical sense to me. How could something invisible help someone in need? But one day, something happened to change my mind.

Angela was only 3 years old when we took our first camping trip together. It was spent in a remote area of the Pocono Mountains of northern Pennsylvania during the last week of August. I woke up very early one morning to go fishing, made some coffee, and headed down to the lake. It was always quiet in early morning, and I loved spending time alone in nature.

About three hours later, I heard someone screaming in the distance. It sounded like my wife Pat, so I raced back to the camper. Pat was hysterically screaming for Angela. Our baby was missing, gone, vanished! Pat had been making breakfast and had turned away from Angela for a second, and during that time Angela must have wandered off.

Many thoughts went through our minds. Was she kidnapped? Was she hurt? How could she have disappeared so quickly without a trace? We decided that I would head in one direction, and Pat would go in the other. We both called for her as we frantically searched everywhere. But we couldn't find her. We called the police, and they were on their way with search helicopters.

Just then, I had an overwhelming feeling to head one more time towards the lake and told Pat to wait at the camper. When I reached the water, I couldn't believe my eyes. There, standing barefoot by the edge of the water, calm as could be, was my little Angela. My heart pounded hard in my chest as I ran to pick her up. She looked dirty but very happy and not at all upset. I asked her where she'd been.

Sweetly and quietly, Angela said she'd been looking for butterflies. She said she followed one into the woods and got lost, but she wasn't afraid. When I asked her why, she said, "Daddy, a nice lady in a white robe came for me, and she looked like a butterfly too!" She said the pretty lady in white told her to follow her to the lake so her daddy could find her. I asked her where the lady in white went after that, and Angela said, "Daddy, she flew up there," and she pointed to the sky.

I was speechless. It was our first time in that campground, and there was no way my baby could have found her way to the lake by herself. The pretty "big butterfly lady" in white was an angel who brought our Angela back safely to us. I'm convinced of it! And now, when Pat talks about angels saving us from harm, I just close my eyes and thank Angela's angel for safely returning her to us that day.

Saved by an Angel
by Sandi A.

In 1997, on the first day of school, my three children and I went to the bus stop. As I chatted with their bus driver, she told me to make sure the children and I looked both ways before crossing the road to get on the bus, because some cars don't stop when they see the bus's yellow flashing lights go on. I thought to myself, "Really?

I thought everybody stops." Then I said good-bye to the driver and waved to my kids, not thinking much more about it.

The next morning, the bus driver came and put on her yellow warning lights; but in my haste, I forgot to look for traffic as I proceeded to cross with my children. We were in a straight line going across the street, and as we all took a step, something happened. It was like I was in a fog and in slow motion. Something stretched out in front of me that felt like an arm. I couldn't walk. I felt a thickness in the air, and it seemed like I was frozen in time. All of a sudden, a minivan flew by us, doing at least 50 miles an hour! Then, as quickly as the fog had formed, it lifted from me and my children, and we all turned to watch the van speed by.

I couldn't believe it! Had we been in that van's path, all four of us could have been killed. I know in my heart that an angel saved us that day. Because I didn't look, the angel stopped all of us from walking out in front of that van. It happened so fast! But it felt like a very long time. In that split second when we were blocked from the path of the speeding van, I felt incredibly warm and loved and supported.

After school that day, I asked my children about what they thought had happened, and they all said they felt the same thing I did. I know now that we must all have a purpose in life. We were saved by our guardian angels for a reason.

A Higher Power
by Debbi S.

In 1990, I attended a Native American Indian retreat with my sister. I have always been drawn to Native American ways—their natural way of healing with herbs, their ability to work with the elements and nature, and the honor and respect they show to wildlife and Mother Earth. My sister and I checked into a room just down the road from the powwow area.

The first day was relaxing and peaceful. We communed with nature and enjoyed the wonderful food and good conversation with others there. In the afternoon of the second day, I was very taken with the mystical feel of the loud drumming; it seemed to penetrate my whole being! That, combined with the incredible Native American dancers, created an ambiance that was both electric and magical.

At the end of that day, my sister and I headed back to our room. My sister was very tired and wanted to stay in and relax, but I wanted to return to the powwow area that evening. At night, the crowds weren't there, and all the Natives camping on the grounds nearby sat around bonfires and told stories, while the young ones danced. I went over toward the main bonfire and sat down, breathing in the smoky cool air.

A striking, tall Native American man with shoulder-length black hair sat down next to me. I recognized him as one of the *fancy* dancers who had performed earlier. For the next hour, he told me about his childhood growing up on a reservation out West. It was sad to hear of the dire poverty and substance abuse that occurred on the reservations. But the most interesting thing he told me was that even children witnessed *spirits* when they were young.

The man was drinking from a bottle wrapped in a brown paper bag. This made me feel uneasy because I knew it was alcohol, and he seemed to be getting a little "too friendly." By the time he finished talking, many of the people at the bonfire had dispersed to go home, leaving only a handful of people sitting around the dying embers.

I stood up and politely excused myself, but he immediately stood up and followed me back on the dark wooded trail—staying about 10 feet behind me. I started walking faster, and so did he. All at once, he ran up behind me, grabbed me, and in a frenzied manner tried to kiss me! Immediately, I said, "No! Don't touch me. I'm married", as I struggled to push him away. But he lunged at me again, and I realized that I was in grave danger. Here I was, a small 5'2" woman with a 6'4", aggressive, intoxicated man—a very hopeless situation! I felt a panic and chill overtake me, and I had a sick feeling in the pit of my stomach, sensing something bad was about to happen.

I said an urgent, silent prayer to God and my angels, asking them to protect me from harm. Instantaneously, I reached up as high as I could and forcefully grabbed the back of the man's arm. I heard myself say, "OK, let's go." And I literally dragged him through the dark woods towards my car. We walked silently, but I was cautious.

I don't know why he allowed this and went along with it, but he did.

About two-thirds of the way down the trail, he told me he had to relieve himself, so I very calmly and slowly released my grip on his arm. As soon as he turned around, I ran for my life! With my heart pounding and my hands shaking, I quickly opened the car door, hopped in and locked the doors. I turned on the ignition, floored the gas pedal, and never looked back. I drove as fast as I could towards the hotel.

My guardian angel was with me, because I could feel a force working through me. It wasn't little me who acted that way in such a tense situation—it was a higher power! I gave thanks to God and the angel and berated myself for being in such a compromising position. My sister and I left the next morning.

About a month later, my sister called and said, "Have you heard the news? The police just captured the powwow dancer you were with that night!" He was at large, moving from state to state because he had murdered three people out West! His most recent crime was horrible. He'd broken into an older widow's house, killed her adult son, and kidnapped her. He drove her across two states, repeatedly raping her. He was on drugs and alcohol. The dear lady finally escaped at a gas station when he left momentarily to pay for gas. He was later charged and sentenced to death by lethal injection.

I am still in shock but also in awe, thinking about how my angel physically worked through me on that ill-fated night. Some unknown force or higher power took over and prompted me to act the way I did—and it probably saved my life!

My Angel of Light
by Catherine G.

I have always considered myself intuitive and sensitive—not at all skeptical or afraid of what's beyond. And so I am open to whatever spiritual experiences might occur in my life. That's why it didn't startle me when, about six years ago, something strange began happening.

Almost everywhere I went, lights began to "flicker" whenever I would pass by. This would always occur outside somewhere but never inside or in my home. Huge highway lights would flicker, and even more often the lights would get much brighter or go out completely when I'd drive by. This happened regularly in parking lots at malls and restaurants, when I drove down highways, and especially at gas stations. It definitely got my attention!

My husband was very skeptical at first because it never happened to him when he was driving alone. But, when I drove alone or with him, these light episodes continued to happen. Most often, it occurred in front of our own house. Whenever I'd glance out the window at the street light, it would start to flicker and either get brighter or dim to a soft glow. No other lamps on our street did this—only the one in front of our house.

I had no explanation for any of this. But then, one night, I had a dream that an *angel of light* came to me. It felt like he was my guardian angel, sent to protect me. I now know that he protects me in the car and surrounds my home with protective light. These light experiences have helped me progress spiritually and have made me more aware of the angelic kingdom and other dimensions of love and light!

Rydell's Healing Presence
by Ray W.

About seven years ago, things started happening that I couldn't explain—events that changed my life forever. The first occurred as I was driving home from work one day.

As I drove, I suddenly heard a male voice telling me to grip the steering wheel with both hands and hold on tight. Too startled to question it, I did what the voice said. Seconds later, the front tire of my truck blew out. If I hadn't had both hands tightly wrapped around the wheel, my truck would have pulled to the left into oncoming traffic. I pulled over and got out of the truck to change the tire. As I changed it, I felt like someone was standing beside me, looking over my shoulder. It was a strange feeling that I'd never had before.

The next day, I was in a bookstore, and a book about angels fell off the shelf and landed at my feet. I laughed to myself and thought,

"Why would I need an angel book?" Well, as it turned out, the book left the store with me, and I started reading it that night. From it, I learned how to meditate and pray. I lit candles, burned incense, and tried for weeks to get in touch with my angel, but nothing happened. I was 50 years old at that time, and, for the previous 30 years, had been a heavy substance abuser.

One day, I felt a very strong urge to try and contact my angel again. I sat down, lit a candle, and started to pray. I must have prayed for about an hour. Then, I noticed that the room had filled with the smell of flowers, and my eyes started to tear. I wasn't crying because of emotions; it felt more like I was shedding cleansing tears. With my eyes still closed, I could see the color purple and then, very plainly, the image of a tall young man. He had long blonde hair, wore a purple robe, and had two very large wings.

He said he was my healing angel, and his name was Rydell—a name I'd never heard of before. He answered all my questions and told me I was healed of substance abuse! Since then, I'm a changed person. My heart has opened up, and I feel love for everyone. My addictions are gone!

From time to time, I feel the presence of other angels that I work with, but it was Rydell who opened the door for my healing. Of course, because God is the one who does the healing, I thank Him every day for sending His healing angel, Rydell, to be with me forever.

Just in Time
by Maureen F.

I was coming home very late one Saturday night, making a 2-hour trip after a social event. I was on a rural road that I drove often; and I knew that at this time of night, it would have little, if any, traffic. It was about 1 a.m. when I came to a crossroad. Since it was so late, I didn't expect anyone to be out, so I was ready to cruise through the intersection without stopping.

Suddenly, something very strange happened. An unknown phenomenon of some kind—a strange force I can't explain—caused my foot to involuntarily hit the brake very hard...so hard I lurched forward in my seat, caught only by the seat belt. Seconds later, an

18-wheeler went whizzing by—a huge truck that somehow came out of nowhere on that desolate, empty road. I had looked both ways and hadn't seen it.

All I know for sure is that it wasn't me who stepped on the brake—and obviously saved my life—that night. There was a power greater than me helping out. And I'm sure it was my angel.

Miraculous Intervention
by Debra C.

I can still vividly remember one ill-fated day when I was a teenager, even though I'm now 52 years old. It was the day my life turned around and my belief in angels began.

I was 14 and on my way to summer school. It was early morning on a July day, and I was walking alone. It seemed like someone was following me, but when I turned around, no one was there. Suddenly, a very large man grabbed me from behind and pushed me up against a nearby brick wall. He had a monstrous look on his face, and he started to tell me what horrible things he was about to do to me.

I felt like I was in a time warp, because when he opened his mouth, I didn't hear anything he was saying. It was as if I'd gone temporarily deaf. Things appeared to be happening in slow motion all around me. Then, the man started to pull me across the street to an overgrown lot, where a vacant house stood.

I tried to yank away, while still gripping my books and my little transistor radio. Just then, I closed my eyes and felt an unknown, yet very powerful presence come over me. I heard myself scream as loudly as I could, "Let go!" When I opened my eyes, the ugly stranger was standing about 15 feet away from me! His arms were down at his sides, and his jaw had dropped open. He looked shocked, and I was stunned because I didn't know what had just happened.

The distance between us gave me a head start to run as fast as I could, so I bolted straight to the school and into the principal's office, where I screamed that a man had just grabbed me. The police arrived a few minutes later, and I rode with them all through the area to try and locate the assailant. He was nowhere in sight.

Back at school, I had to attend classes even though I was still terrified. But soon I felt strangely calm. When school let out, I camouflaged myself in the crowd and ran home a different way. That evening, I thought about the events of the day and realized that something extraordinary had happened. Some power—greater than I—had intervened. An angel had blessed me with a miraculous intervention that would change my life and belief system forever!

Thanks, Nancy
by Dawn C.

When I was a child, I had a best friend named Nancy. We would do everything together, and we vowed we would always stay together. Then, when she was only 10, Nancy died in a tragic accident. Since then, I've had a strong feeling that she is one of my spirit angels because I feel her presence frequently.

About three years ago, my two sons, Zachary and Dallas, had an opportunity to go to South Carolina with their uncles and their families. At first, my husband and I were all for it; but two weeks before they were to leave, I started to get a bad feeling about the trip. As the trip got closer, I became more and more upset. And for some unexplainable reason, I just couldn't shake the bad feeling.

My husband began to get angry with me. My sister, Michelle, told me to tell the boys how I felt and let them decide if they still wanted to go. They decided to make the trip, and I reluctantly dropped them off at my brother-in-law Timmy's place and kissed them good-bye. As I drove away, I said, "Nancy, you're my special angel, and I know you're here with me. I need you to go with Zack and Dallas on this trip and watch over them." I soon felt better, though I was still a little apprehensive.

About midnight, my brother-in-law Joey called to say they were safe and almost to their destination. The boys were riding in their Uncle Timmy's car, and Uncle Joey was following right behind them. We hung up, but I couldn't get back to sleep. I still felt uneasy, like something was wrong. A couple of hours later, I finally drifted off to sleep.

Suddenly, I was awakened by the phone ringing. It was 3 a.m. I answered, not by saying hello but by saying, "What happened?" It was Joey, and he said, "Dawn, calm down. After I hung up with you, we were in a bad car accident. The boys, who were riding with Tim, had to go to the bathroom and decided to switch cars and ride with me. My car was the one that got hit. The good news is the boys are OK."

I breathed a huge sigh of relief. Joey said it was a miracle that Zack and Dallas were unharmed. His car had been rear-ended by a large truck while my boys were asleep in the back seat. The police said that, because they were sleeping and their bodies were very relaxed, they were like rag dolls at the time of impact and were better able to handle the crushing blow. They were pulled from the car without a scratch on them!

To this day, I believe that my special angel, Nancy, was with my boys in the car when the accident happened, and I will go to my grave believing that. I thanked her again and again that night for protecting Zack and Dallas. You see, Nancy was my boys' age when she was killed by a drunken, off-duty cop. She was standing on a median strip waiting to cross a busy road. Upon impact, she never knew what hit her. She was a fun-loving little girl, full of energy. And I know that now she's a spirit keeping other little girls and boys safe from harm during accidents!

Note from Michele*: True angels have never been human souls. Many of us believe our departed friends or relatives watch over us like angels—and they do. However, a "protective soul", as in the case of Nancy, is correctly referred to as a "spirit guide."*

Angelic Occurrences
by Ellen B.

When my mom died after a long illness, my oldest daughter, Mary Ellen, was only 7 years old. She was extremely close to my mom, as was I. Towards the end of her life, my mom's whole world was my two girls. I truly believe they were what kept her going during the entire last year of her life.

A few weeks after my mom's death, Mary Ellen began telling me stories about encounters she was having with my mom. Once in the middle of the night, she woke up and saw a ball of white light in her room. Coming from the ball of light, she heard unbelievably beautiful angelic voices—like nothing she'd ever heard before. She said she received a message saying that you can't always ask God for all his strength because God needs that power to send angels down to Earth.

Mary Ellen was also told that an angel's powers are different in Heaven than they are on Earth. She told me my mom was coming to her at night and comforting her. This all made perfect sense because for weeks I'd been shocked by how well Mary Ellen was handling my mom's death— much better than I was! Now I knew why…Mom had been coming to visit her!

On another occasion, while in her room, Mary Ellen had a momentary glimpse of white angel robes from the corner of her eye. Later, she told me about an incident at school when drops of holy water fell from the air onto her hands. She believed it was my mom getting her attention because my mom was a teacher in my school district for years. I have no idea how Mary Ellen, at the age of 7, knew it was holy water that my mom sent. But she has always *known* things ...things that I can't put into words.

Other family members have also had contact with my mom since she died, but I feel so comforted to know that she is with God's angels in Heaven and that she took the time to communicate with my special little Mary Ellen.

Comments from Michele

I would like to conclude this chapter with two stories of angelic encounters from a very dear friend of mine. In 1995, my husband, Jon, and I built a large new home. The next year, I was looking for a dependable and capable person to help me maintain it, and I hired a very special lady named Ruth. When Ruth first walked into my entrance foyer to be interviewed for the position, I saw "light" all around her. She emanated a glowing, childlike joy that was attractive and infectious. I could tell she loved people, loved life, and had a very good heart.

Ruth was a dedicated mother of six as well as a grandmother. I later learned that she could also *see* angels. Never having volunteered the fact that I communicate with angels, I was surprised when one day Ruth relayed to me some true stories of encounters she had with angels in my home. When I was compiling information for this book, I asked Ruth if she would be willing to share a couple of stories about her experiences. She thought about it and was very sincere in her answer. She hadn't told many people about her gift of being able to view the angelic realms, but she considered me a friend and decided she'd be willing to share the ones that happened at my home. I hope you enjoy them.

A Piece of Heaven
by Ruth C.

From the time I was very small, I have been able to *see* angels—wings and all—the most beautiful beings I've ever seen! One sunny afternoon, I was cleaning Michele's master bedroom and looked over at the bathroom door. The door lit up and seemed to sparkle. I opened the door, and, instead of a bathroom, what I saw looked like a "piece of Heaven." There were no walls, floor, or ceiling—just a large space filled with angels!

As I stood watching, the heavenly host was revealed to me, with both male and female angels flying around, wearing white. There were also different gemstones of all colors that sparkled around them. The angels looked like ones I've seen in old paintings. I knew they could see me, but they didn't talk. It was like Jesus was showing me a piece of the *divine realm,* where there was no pain and no worries, just peace and love. I watched this scene for a very long time and then closed the door. The only people I told about it were Michele and my daughter, who was working with me that day.

The Rooftop Angels
by Ruth C.

Another occurrence happened in the summertime, about two years later. When I arrived at Michele's house with my cleaning partner, I happened to look up at the roof. There in the sky were the largest angels I've ever seen flying around the top of the house. I knew somehow that Michele wasn't home—the angels seemed to be protecting everything.

When we walked around to the back door, there was a note saying that Michele and her husband Jon were away in Virginia. Two weeks later, when I told Michele what I saw, she seemed comforted. She told me that during the trip she had become seriously ill and ended up in a Virginia hospital. Michele was happy to hear that angels were protecting their home while they were gone.

I also want to say that Michele is one of the most loving, sincere, caring, and beautiful people I know. I'm not surprised that the angels are watching over her family, pets, and home.

Note from Michele: *This morning, I was editing stories for this book and read Ruth's accounts. As I did, a warmth came over me, and I glanced at the wall. There were rainbow sparkles everywhere—a confirmation showing us that angels indeed surround us.*

PART II

DEPARTED LOVED ONES

Chapter Two

Dream Communications

"A sweet thing, for whatever time,
to revisit in dreams the dear dead we have lost." – Euripides

There are many ways that a departed spirit from the fourth dimension communicates. The most common way is through dreams. When you dream of a loved one who has passed, your soul is out of your body and is on the astral plane meeting with that person's soul on the other side. The dream is usually simple—the spirit may just smile, nod at you, or extend a hand, without any form of thought communication. Your loved one may also say just a word or sentence to communicate a thought form. They are communicating with you *telepathically* or mind to mind, rather than verbally. The following dreams I've had illustrate how a simple message from my dad and stepsister changed the course of my life.

Do It on Your Own

My father, Lear, passed away suddenly from a brain tumor in 1966. I was born when he was 50 and was his only child—the "apple of his eye." I started to draw and paint at the age of 3 and started formal art lessons in the first grade. The lessons ultimately led to my first "one-man show" in sixth grade—something my dad was very proud of. He always boasted about my creative talent.

When I was 14, my dad transitioned to the "other side," and I painted a self-portrait in his honor. In the painting, I was around age 12 and holding a gentle fawn. My dad always loved the name Susan, and since I painted the portrait in his honor, I titled it "Brown-eyed Susan." Later, I designed porcelain collectors' plates for a nationally known company, and that company was interested in reproducing my "Brown-eyed Susan" on collector plates. The original painting was then crated and sent to a dealer in Texas for evaluation.

A few months passed, and I was unable to contact the dealer and became nervous that my painting had been lost forever. One night, I had a lucid dream of my dad. He stood in front of me, wearing his favorite sport shirt, and placed his hands firmly on my shoulders. He shook his head "no" and simply sent the message, "Don't sell or give your artwork to any dealer—you do it on your own!"

I took his advice because I knew Dad was looking out for my welfare. A friend and I flew to Texas and tracked down the dealer. He turned out to be quite a seedy character, but I was able to recover my original piece of artwork and bring it home.

From then on, I "did it on my own" as my dad had suggested. I started my own art business and sold my own work exclusively. The dream confirmed for me that souls still love us and watch over us when they pass. They know and care about what happens in our lives here on the earth-plane. I've only had three dreams of my dad in almost 40 years. But each time, the dream has been vivid, and he has given me very specific advice for my welfare.

I Like It Here

My stepsister Dorris was 20 when I was born, and she was on the verge of graduating from college. Dorris was very bright and independent, but we never totally bonded emotionally because of our age difference. She never had children, but she owned and bred beautiful show dogs. Toward the end of her life, Dorris became disillusioned with the world in general. She was diagnosed with breast cancer at age 46 and had a very painful death a decade later at

56. I prayed for her soul, because, although she believed in angels, she didn't embrace any form of an afterlife.

A few months after Dorris' passing, I had a poignant dream. In the dream, I was standing in a long hallway filled with bright light. I started to walk down the hallway, and I noticed white doors on the left and right of me. As I continued to walk, something prompted me to open a door on my right. When I did, I saw a room illuminated with the brightest light I'd ever seen. There was a large picture window through which more light was streaming, and in front of the window was the silhouette of a woman.

I gently asked, "Dorris, is that you?" The woman slowly turned around, and indeed it was my stepsister, looking very young and vibrant—about the age of 30. She smiled and simply said, "I like it here!" I woke up knowing that indeed Dorris was in the light of God. She had arrived safely and liked her new spiritual environment. This experience taught me to believe in the power of prayer. I encourage my readers to pray for their departed loved ones, as well as those who still remain on the earth-plane.

The following stories are about special communiqués from loved ones through dreams.

Drink More Water
by Shelby G.

A couple of years ago, I had a very enlightening dream. I was in my living room sitting across from my Aunt Fran. She was named after my mother's mother, Frances. Aunt Fran had passed away suddenly when I was just 8 years old, and I didn't remember much about her. In fact, in the dream, I was very surprised to see her! She was wearing a light blue dress and looked young and very happy.

Suddenly, Aunt Fran looked directly at me and simply said, "Drink more water!" And, with that, I woke up. It was so vivid, and yet the dream left me very confused. Aunt Fran was my mother's sister; and surely, if the dream meant anything, my mother could help me piece things together. So, the next day, I called my mother and asked her what she thought.

My mother seemed surprised that I'd ever even dream of Aunt Fran. But, as she thought about it, she started to unravel the mysterious dream. Aunt Fran was found dead in her living room when she was quite young. She had been diagnosed with a rare kidney disease, and my mother remembered the doctor telling her to drink lots of steam-distilled water (which they had to boil) to cleanse her kidneys. My mother also remembered that Aunt Fran had been buried in a light blue dress.

But I still didn't get it. Why would Aunt Fran come and tell me to drink more water? Six months later, I found out why. I had developed a severe urinary tract infection and was put on antibiotics. The last thing the doctor advised me to do was to *drink more water*. In fact, he said that for my condition, steam-distilled water would be the best!

It seems strange, but now I know in my heart that Aunt Fran was just looking out for me. It was a precognition dream that helped me get through a frustrating and painful time in my life. You never know who the helpful messenger is going to be—you just need to be open to all possibilities!

The Heavenly Dance
by Heidi L.

A very dear male friend of mine passed away 15 years ago. Since then, I have had many dreams about him, but one stands out in my mind. He passed very quickly, and I prayed for his soul to get situated over there and be at peace.

About a year after he passed, I had my first lucid dream of him. It felt like I was suspended in a "way station" between dimensions. I was in a large, beautiful ballroom, with white marble floors and pillars, and a sparkling glass elevator. I was standing in the middle of the room when the elevator doors slowly opened. My handsome friend was standing there wearing a tuxedo. He approached me, smiled, and extended his hand.

The next thing I knew, I was wearing an elegant chiffon ball gown. We were floating in the air dancing to "I Could Have Danced All Night" with an orchestra playing in the background. I discovered later that this was a melody from "My Fair Lady," a movie I never saw in its entirety. It made sense this song would be playing, because my friend loved Broadway plays and musicals.

One of the verses says, "I could have spread my wings and done a thousand things I've never done before. I'll never know what made it so exciting, when all at once my heart took flight. I only know when he began to dance with me, I could have danced, danced, danced all night!" And that's exactly how I felt! I spun around, and when I turned to face him, he was gone. He just disappeared ...and I was alone.

The elevator doors once again opened, and this time it was an African-American woman in a white business suit. She was wearing glasses and looked very professional, but she seemed upset and somewhat frantic. She approached me and asked me where my friend was. I told her that he'd left and gone back upstairs. She turned and started walking back to the elevator, but I heard her say as she walked away, "Good! He's not supposed to be down here this long." Then I woke up.

The melody stayed in my head the entire day, and I still hear it every now and then and have visions of the dance. I know that my friend came down to meet me for one last dance, but he couldn't stay too long because he probably had work to do in Heaven. It was just the most wonderful experience I can remember!

Reconnections from the Past
by Raymond P.

Several years ago, I had an experience concerning a certain dream. The dream involved a family of four children who lived across the street from me when I was young. The oldest child was my age, and he and I were best friends. The youngest child, Billy, was 10 years younger than me. I often baby-sat for Billy when he was 5 and 6 years old, and I felt very protective towards him.

Billy's family later moved to another state, and I lost contact with him. For years, I heard rumors that Billy had a drug problem and had been in trouble with the law. My thoughts were with him, and I always wished him well in my mind. In my dream, I was standing outside of the house I grew up in. I looked over at my neighbor's house across the street and saw that their back kitchen door was opening. Each family member left the house one by one, in single file. Each one looked over at me and waved, and I waved back. I found it strange that their youngest son, Billy, wasn't with them.

The day after I had that dream, my parents came to my house for Easter Sunday dinner. Upon arriving, my dad informed me that Billy had committed suicide by shooting himself in the head three days before. I was stunned, and this news sent chills down my spine! I think Billy wanted to let me know he had left his family behind on Earth, and that I should contact them, which I did.

They were glad to receive my condolences, concern, and support. Even though Billy didn't appear to me in the dream, it gave his family comfort to know I dreamt of them at a time when they needed to hear that someone cared.

Miracle of My Birth
by Charlie H.

I think I remember the "other side" before I was born. When I was very young, I had a recurring dream:

> My mother and I were walking in a beautiful, heavenly field. She was young and lovely, and I was small enough that I had to raise my arm high over my shoulder just to hold her hand. I viewed the scene from an aerial vantage point above and behind. Everything was perfect, peaceful, warm, and loving. Then we came to a high cliff, and we stopped. There were train tracks that stretched over a gorge to a ledge on the other side. There was no bridge, only tracks—two iron rails with cross ties. When I glanced down over the edge, I saw a river far below as if from a pinpoint perspective. We just stood there looking ahead in silence. I *felt* a "loving presence" ask me if I was ready this time to take the journey *and* if I was sure. It was not really a voice; it was more like a simple *understanding*. I nodded "yes," and my mother and I started to walk down the tracks.
>
> Just then, a train headed toward us as we were in the middle of the tracks. The rumble grew louder, and the tracks shook as the train headed straight for us. My anxiety grew with the deafening roar and vibration. My mother and I lay down and clung desperately to

a railroad tie as the train passed so close overhead. It was all very scary, so I just hung on for dear life.

Things soon calmed down, and the haze cleared. I remember standing up and looking around for my mother, and, at first, she was not there. When I looked again, I saw her. We again held hands and walked the rest of the way down the tracks together. It was an exhilarating and exciting new feeling, breathing fresh air into my lungs. It felt like a new beginning, a new life. I am now 50 years old, but I can still sense the *feeling* of that new beginning, and I can still *feel* the love from that initial question, "Are you ready this time?"

My mother has a rare blood type, and my parents had Rh factor problems with childbirth. She's had many losses— two miscarriages, a stillborn child, and a daughter who lived only a few hours. My mother had 17 blood transfusions giving birth to me. She says that, with the stillborn birth, she had a near-death experience in which she was walking down a long stretch of train tracks! When she reached the end, her father was standing there, shaking his head "no," so she turned around and came back.

She is still alive with me today. People talk about the tunnel or connecting portal between the dimensions. For us, it was the train tracks that seemed to lead us from one side (or dimension) to the other. I know that my mother's first miscarriage was my soul changing its mind and going back. Now, this time, I was ready to make the journey to Earth.

Communicating with Numbers
by Lucy H.

A few years after my father passed away, I had a vivid dream about him. In the dream, I was in a hospital room with my father, and my husband was on an operating table holding his chest. The doctors were standing over my husband, but they couldn't see my dad—only I could. My dad handed me a card from a jukebox, and printed on it in bold letters was the number, **104**. I thought at first that this was because Dad would always have breakfast in a certain diner and would sometimes play the jukebox. But the amazing thing is that now I realize that the number 104 has played such a big part in my life.

A couple of months after the dream, my husband had a congenital heart problem and thought he was having a heart attack. We rushed him to the hospital, and he ended up in room 104! Then, my music partner and I were signed to a recording contract that came out of the blue. The number assigned to our CD on an Internet site began with 104.

Next, my teenage daughter became pregnant and delivered my first grandson at 1:04 a.m. Soon after, I was given a great opportunity to further my work in January 2004 (1-04). In addition, I often see the number 104 on car license plates when I'm driving and on digital clocks when I'm prompted to glance at them. Most interesting of all, since Dad was the one who showed me the 104, is that my father's birthday was October 4th (10-4).

Now, whenever I see that number, I say, "Hi, Dad! How ya doin'?" And I know that he's never really left me. He's still there all the time, watching me from the other side.

My Vision of Mother
by Lucy W.

My mother Joanne was a beautiful woman who died far too young—at the age of 52—from a heart condition and complications of diabetes, which she'd had all her life. At that time, I was 24, married, and pregnant with twins. My mother's unexpected death was the greatest shock of my life. The saddest part was I never got to say good-bye to her.

My mother knew I was having twin boys, so she asked me to name one of them after my father, Frank. So, after they were born, I honored that request and called one of them Frankie. They were wonderful boys. Seven years later, I delivered an adorable baby girl, and I named her Joanne, after my mother.

Soon after baby Joanne was born, I had a vision. It was as real and lucid as if it was happening right now. Here's what happened: I was asleep on my back, and I distinctly remember opening my eyes and seeing a beautiful face hovering above me. I looked closer and saw that it was my mother! It was just her face, not her body, and it was glowing and surrounded with pure, white light. She was smiling at me and looked joyful and peaceful. I said, "Mom, is that you?" And she nodded but didn't say a word. Then she was gone.

Warmth enveloped me, and I felt an overwhelming sense of peace and contentment. I believe that vision was my mother's way of acknowledging baby Joanne and saying both thank-you and good-bye. She let me know with just one glance that she saw all her grandchildren, even though she had died before they were born. This vision happened 8 years after she died, and she must have loved us very much to bring down that much energy and appear to me. I will miss her until the day I die, but I know she'll be waiting for me in Heaven …and we can then be together again!

Comforting Dreams
by Kathryn M.

My husband died very suddenly, leaving me to raise our young son alone. Our first wedding anniversary after he died was the most difficult for me, because it fell on Mother's Day that year. I was feeling very alone and in need of comfort. Interestingly, that night, I had a very reassuring dream…

In the dream, I saw my best friend's mother, who had passed away several years before. She looked radiantly beautiful and wore a long pale blue dressing gown. She was happily perched on the end of a bed in a bedroom I didn't recognize. I looked straight at her and asked her if she could see me. She nodded "yes."

Then, I asked her if she could see her daughter, and she again nodded "yes." My next question was about my dear husband. I asked her if my husband was with her, and she shook her head "yes" and pointed over to the left. Immediately, I felt myself being pulled at an incredible speed in the direction she pointed—I felt like I was being transported into another dimension!

Then just as suddenly I stopped! And my husband's face appeared before me. It looked like there was a bright new white snow behind him, and he appeared younger—about 30 years old and healthy. He acknowledged me with a very warm smile, looked at me knowingly and very lovingly, and extended his hand. Then, he simply said to me, "Kathryn, you're doing fine!" With that, he waved good-bye and disappeared. I heard him call my name three times, and I woke up from the dream.

The next day, my son came home from school and excitedly told me about a dream he had the night before. He said it was very real to him, and his dad was in it. In his dream, his dad smiled and waved at him and said, "You're doing just fine!" Then, he called my son's name three times and disappeared, and my son woke up.

We experienced the same dream on the same night! I felt it was a wonderful gift and a true miracle! Those dreams made me a total believer that a person's spirit lives on after death. And I take comfort in knowing that my husband watches over us and wants us to be "just fine."

Dad's Watching Over Us
by Lisa D.

My father died about 10 years ago, when he was just 55. The pain of his death was so intense that it literally left me unable to cry or grieve in any "normal" way. Life went on, and when I got married, I tried not to think about my father not being there to walk me down the aisle and asked my brother to escort me.

A couple of years after we were married, my husband and I discussed starting a family. Unfortunately, our first three attempts ended in miscarriage, and my heart was shipwrecked. Finally, I became pregnant again and gave birth to a baby boy—my little Charlie who just turned 4. Charlie's an exceptional child, and when he was barely 2, a strange event happened.

I didn't have any photos of my father displayed around the house, because they were too painful for me to look at. But on this particular day I was going through some old family photos. As I sorted through them, a photo of my dad fell out of the pile, and little Charlie picked it up. He said, "There's Grandpa Frank!" Of course, he'd never seen or known his Grandpa, so I asked him—through my tears—how he knew that was his Grandpa, let alone that his name was Frank.

Charlie said to me, "I see him, Mommy." From that moment on, I started to grieve. Though I had been quite emotional whenever I thought of my dad over the years, I had never fully grieved his loss. It was no mistake that Charlie was telling me to move through that process, and I felt strongly that he was guided by my father.

Since that day, I've had many experiences and dreams involving both my dad and my dear grandmother, who'd passed away earlier. Recently, my dad came to me in a dream and stood before me with a small boy on his shoulders. Dad told me to let go, that everything was fine now, and that he is with my son—the baby I'd lost just before Charlie was born. The doctors had told me that the third baby I miscarried was a boy; they hadn't been able to tell the gender of the other two. Dad called my baby "Sean."

The dream was so real and loving that I forgave the Universe for taking my dad and my son. I've also begun working with hospice patients and am no longer afraid to live life to the fullest. I now know for sure that Dad is watching over me and my family, and that gives me great peace.

Boomer's Good-bye
by M.C. P.

Animals have always been a big part of my life. In fact, many times I've been closer to animals than to humans. I've read books about deceased relatives communicating through dreams, but my gift is making connections with animals that have passed over.

For example, I had worked for a pet-sitting company for 18 months and had a regular group of 14 animals that I tended to daily. Before I resigned in 2001, I had a couple weeks to soak up unconditional love from my critter friends. My favorite puppy was a darling 8-month-old Vizsla named "Boomer." His sparkling light green human-like eyes, coupled with his stellar red coat and energetic spirit, made him a very special dog in my heart.

During my last week on the job, I wasn't scheduled to visit Boomer, so I never got a chance to say "good-bye" to him. Three weeks later, I awoke on a Saturday morning from a very vivid dream. In the dream, I was traveling to my parents' house to care for Boomer because he was staying overnight there. When I arrived, I was greeted by a smiling, bouncy, and healthy little "Boomie." He looked just like the cherished photos that I have of him. He proceeded to give me lots of kisses; and, when I held him, I plainly felt his soft, velvety fur and his wet nose pressed against mine.

That very morning, I had the strongest urge to call his owners, but I thought I'd wait until later that day. At 3 p.m., the owner of the pet-sitting company called, which took me by surprise. Sue said, in a shaking voice, "M.C., I think you should know this—Boomer died last night." Instantly, my body began to shiver with chills. I was stunned, horrified and then mystified. I choked back the tears as I said to Sue, "I dreamt of Boomer just last night!"

Later, I sat down and gathered my thoughts. All our family pets have gone to my parents' house to die. They have returned to the homestead for a backyard burial. I knew that Boomer had come to me to say "good-bye" and to let me know that he had safely passed over. I felt I needed to forward the message to his owners, so I wrote his folks a letter and shared with them the details of the dream. I relayed how bouncy, healthy, and happy "Boomie" appeared. I also told them how much joy their little guy brought me daily—the beaming smile I had when I was with him.

Needless to say, I felt so much better after writing to them ... because that's what Boomer inspired me to do!

Mother's Helping Hand
by Linda M.

My mother, who was a proud collector of many fine objects, died very suddenly in November 2003. After her death, I began the overwhelming task of cleaning out her house. Because she had been a collector for so many years, it was difficult to decide which of the pieces in her wonderful collections to keep and which to give away or throw away.

One day during the cleanup, my 14-year-old daughter blurted out, "Maybe Grams herself could tell us!" A few of us had moved into her house to start the clearing-out process, and I was sleeping in my mother's room. One night, in the midst of our frustration about what to keep, I had a very clear dream in which many of our family members appeared. My mother was also in the dream, looking much younger and healthier, and bursting with energy. My mother said, "Don't worry, Linda. I'm going to help you clean the house."

The next morning, I couldn't wait to tell my daughter and my sister-in-law what I had dreamt. But, before I could say anything, my daughter ran up to me and said, "Guess what, Mom? Grams was in my dream last night, and she told me that she's gonna help us clean the house!" Moments later, my sister-in-law came down the steps and said, "Linda! I dreamt about your mother last night. She was wearing a shirt with the sleeves rolled up and said she'll be helping us with the house."

I stood there wide-eyed with my mouth open. All three of us had had the same dream on the same night! It was my mother's way of letting us know everything would be alright. Her love, her support, and her helping hand were there for us. I realized that all we had to do was ask for her help, and she was ready to give it. And, from then on, our decisions about what to do with mother's things seemed effortless.

The Blue Candle
by Susan T.

The year 1982 was devastating for our family because we experienced three deaths within just five months. Aunt Joan was my mother's sister, and she was the last of the three to die from cancer that year. I was close to her and missed her a lot.

A couple weeks after her death, I had a vision that I was in Heaven. It was a place filled with light, with no ceiling or floor. I was floating among beautiful green plants, which I was tending. My Aunt Joan loved gardening and plants too, and soon I felt her energy.

Suddenly, she appeared before me, looking radiantly beautiful. Her hair was perfectly coiffed, and she wore a long white, sleeveless dress with a V-shaped neckline. A graceful white cape was attached at her shoulders and flowed behind her. In each hand, she held a light blue candle. One had a royal blue stripe down the side of it, and the other was solid blue.

I told Aunt Joan I wanted to light the striped candle, but she said, "No, Susan, that's my candle. I light it when I'm praying for those left on the earth-plane." I must have looked sad, because she continued, "You must light the solid blue candle and pray for those who have passed over here." Just as she finished giving me that instruction, a match appeared in my hand, so I proceeded to light the blue candle while praying for all my relatives who were in Heaven.

At that moment, my phone rang and woke me up from my dream. It was my sister telling me that my grandmother (my father's mother) had just died. The clock said 5 a.m. It was interesting that, even though Aunt Joan wasn't close to my dad's side of the family, she told me in the dream to pray for all my relatives who'd crossed over.

I kept the dream to myself, telling no one about it. Although it was a beautiful experience, it was also somewhat confusing. I prayed for a confirmation that indeed I had visited Joan and should continue to light blue candles for those who've passed. Well, about a week later, I got my confirmation.

My mother called to say something unusual had happened. My Aunt Donna (her other sister) had a strange experience with her son Brian, who was 10. The night before, when she'd tucked Brian in at bedtime and was about to kiss him goodnight, he said, "Mom, did you see Aunt Joan standing in my room?" Donna was surprised and said, "No, Brian. Aunt Joan is dead." But Brian insisted: "Mom, she was standing right here, wearing a long white dress, and she smiled at me. And in her hand was a little blue candle."

There was my confirmation! Someone once told me that if a dream is a true vision, you will never forget it. It has been 21 years since I dreamt of Aunt Joan, and it is still as vivid as if I dreamt of her this morning. Now, when someone dies, I always light a blue candle for that person, and I pray he or she will be in peace and in the light of God.

Good News
by Sharyn W.

I am a 58-year-old wife, mother of two, and grandmother of three, and I have always been very close to my family. Over the last 10 years, I have become much more open to the realm of the spiritual, although I had never had a paranormal experience. That changed one night soon after my mother died.

My mother passed away very suddenly on October 17, 1991. She was only 68 at the time, so it was a shock to everyone in our family. I never dreamt of her before she died, but I had a prophetic dream about her a couple of months after she passed. In the dream, I was standing outside on a bright sunny day, enjoying the weather. Beside me was our son and daughter-in-law, Deb.

I glanced over at Deb and noticed that she didn't look well, and she felt cold to the touch. I ran inside the house and grabbed a blanket to wrap around her. Deb and my son sat down on a nearby bench. I proceeded to walk down the street—through the neighborhood. Then I noticed a house with a bright blue door. The door slowly opened, and my mother came out to greet me. I was so happy to see her. She looked wonderful—so beautiful, healthy, and serene! I reached out to touch her, but she merely said, "I can't stay. Take care of Deb—she's pregnant!" And, at that point, I woke up.

The dream was so clear and bright, I knew somehow it must be real. That morning was Sunday, so I went to church. The last hymn of the service was my mother's favorite—the one that was played at her funeral. Our church has never played that hymn at a regular service before, and I took it as a sign that my mother had indeed communicated with me the night before.

I told my husband and my sister about the dream, and they were happy I'd heard from Mother. My daughter-in-law had been trying to get pregnant for five years, so I resisted telling my son and her about the dream. I didn't want to get their hopes up in case it wasn't true.

About a month later, my son invited us over for Sunday dinner. As soon as we arrived, he blurted out, "Guess what! Deb's pregnant!" He was so proud and happy! I almost fell over when he told me, and you should have seen the look on my husband's face. We were both thrilled. A few months later, Deb delivered a healthy and precious baby boy. He was our first grandchild, and his great-grandmother had been the one who first brought us the "good news" about his arrival!

Heavenly Hide and Seek
by Kim S.

The first gift my husband gave me when we were dating was a gorgeous emerald ring. It was very expensive, and I adored it. I wore it for many years—well into our marriage—until one day, I realized I had lost it. I searched our house, our yard, my car—everywhere I could think of—but I never found it.

Years went by, and eventually we sold our house. I thought about the ring and about leaving the house—and maybe the ring—behind. It made me feel sad. Hoping against hope, I figured that maybe as we were cleaning out the house to pack our things, the ring would turn up; but it never did.

In the meantime, my precious mother died very suddenly. She too loved jewelry, and I wondered if maybe she could help me find my ring—from Heaven! I asked her for her help, and then I waited patiently for a sign. A few months after we were settled into our new house, my emerald ring started coming back into my thoughts.

Then, one Sunday morning, I had an unusual dream in which a female voice (which sounded very much like my mother) told me the following: "Go to the attic and look in the box of jeans. Look in the pocket of the jeans, and you'll find the ring." I immediately awoke, went up to the attic, and found myself drawn to one particular box that we had moved ...but never opened.

Inside the box, on the very top, was a pair of old jeans my brother-in-law had given me to work in around the house. I looked in the pocket of the jeans, and there was my emerald ring! I was so amazed that I thought I was still dreaming! I couldn't believe it! How had my ring gotten into that pocket? Then it occurred to me...

I had worn those jeans one day at the old house when I was washing the kitchen floor. I must have put the ring in the pocket then and had never washed the jeans. In fact, I didn't even remember packing them. But, here they were, and here was my ring! I knew right away that my mother had helped me find the emerald ring because sentimental things, like special pieces of jewelry, were very important to her. Through my tears of joy, I said a silent prayer to thank her.

Grandmother Mary's Wisdom
by Mary D.

Of all my family members, Grandma Mary and I were the closest. She was a good listener and counselor, so I would always go to her for advice. In essence, she was a very wise woman.

After her passing, whenever I needed help, she would appear to me in my dreams. Each time, she would project in a blue flowered dress and white apron—her favorite outfit for cooking. In one particular dream, Grandma Mary specifically told me that a precious little girl would enter my life. This really confused me because I was no longer capable of having children. My daughter and I had been estranged for years, so the thought of a little girl in my life was quite surprising.

I was working two full-time jobs at that time, to make ends meet. But one day I had an urgent "feeling" NOT to go to either job, so I called in sick—something that I would normally never do. While I was home that day, a registered letter came for me. I couldn't imagine whom it was from, so I quickly opened it. I then realized it was for my estranged daughter (she and I have the same name).

The letter was from an adoption agency that claimed to have a baby girl who was actually my daughter's natural child—my granddaughter! I started to cry because no one in our family knew the child existed, not even the birth father. The agency listed her name as Rachael—a beautiful name—and said she was a year old.

I was so shaken by this news that I didn't know what to do. I prayed about it and finally decided I should call a good attorney to win custody of my granddaughter, Rachael. That was the beginning of an exhausting and difficult ordeal. I was fighting not only the adoption agency but also my daughter and the family that was in the process of adopting her. But I couldn't quit!

The courts finally ruled in my favor, and my beautiful, sweet Rachael came home with me. I know now that it was my Grandma Mary who intervened and prompted me to stay home from work that day, 12 years prior, so I could receive that registered letter. Her guidance, wisdom, and protection gave me the precious gift of a little girl! And for that I am forever grateful.

A Special Farewell
by Kathy I.

For many years I've enjoyed my hair dressing profession and had many wonderful clients. One in particular I became very close to. Her name was Antoinette, and she was a dear little Italian lady. I felt like I was her surrogate granddaughter and we shared so much over the years. At age 94, she still had beautiful hair and a glowing complexion. I had a vivid dream about her on the Saturday morning of Memorial Day weekend, 2004. First, I heard my name, Kathy, being called. Though I was still sleeping, it seemed my soul had left my body and was standing directly behind my bed. I saw myself sit up in bed and look to a huge wingback chair. Sitting in the chair was my dear client, Antoinette! She smiled and softly said, "Kathy, I've come to say goodbye. It's time for me to go; I'll be seeing you."

This communication was done telepathically. She was flanked by relatives, on each side of her chair, and one of them took her arm and helped her to get up. She slowly walked over to me, looked into my eyes, took my hands, and once again said, "Goodbye."

When I awoke from the vision I knew I would never see her again physically in this lifetime. I glanced at my digital clock and it was 2:45 a.m. The next day was Sunday and my boyfriend and I went to a barbecue picnic. On the way home I turned off the car radio and said to him that I would never see Antoinette again. He acted like he didn't believe me. But as soon as I walked in my front door and turned on the answering machine, there was a message from Antoinette's daughter, Rose. When I called Rose back I shared my vision and she confirmed that her mother indeed had passed away at 2:45 a.m. Sunday morning! She also confided that that morning she had prayed to God for a "sign" that her mother was happy and in

Heaven with the other relatives. My vision was the sign she needed to feel at peace in her time of need. I felt so honored that Antoinette appeared to me, and chose me to be her messenger.

The following Tuesday evening I went to the funeral parlor to do Antoinette's hair. When I saw the dress she was wearing I froze— her daughter had bought that special dress for her on Monday, and it was the exact same dress she was wearing when she appeared to say goodbye!

This was the most profound spiritual experience I've ever had. It has reaffirmed my faith in an afterlife and I am confident that many of my friends, relatives, and clients will be there to receive me when it's my time to say farewell to the earth plane.

Chapter Three

Clairvoyance (Seeing)

"What beck'ning spirit, along the moonlight shade
Invites my steps and points to yonder glade?" – Alexander Pope

Clairvoyance means "clear seeing or vision." When I'm doing consultations, the primary way I work is to use my "visionary" abilities to *see* the spirit first. Most individuals *feel* or *hear* spirits before they see them. Clairvoyance comes with *seeing* with the "third eye" rather than physically. The third eye is located between, and about an inch above, the eyebrows. A spirit from the fourth dimension needs to store energy and lower its frequency in order to be *seen*. The following stories contain apparitions or sightings of departed loved ones. The first one happened to my husband and me in August of 2003, when we were enjoying a two-week European river cruise on the River Rhine.

Waiting in the Station

We started the cruise from Basel, Switzerland, traveling to quaint towns throughout Germany, France, and Holland, finally ending our adventure in Amsterdam. While visiting the Netherlands, we literally "went back in time" when we visited an historic, turn-of-the-century village, complete with authentic windmills, farms, livestock, and stores. The site is to the Netherlands what Williamsburg, Virginia is to the United States.

The village was spread across hundreds of acres of land, so we needed to ride a little train to see all the sights. Since it was an overcast day with scattered showers, the village wasn't very crowded. As we pulled into one of the little train stations, my husband and I glanced to the right. There, standing in the station, looking directly at us was my husband's brother-in-law, Bill! We both gasped, because he was only a few feet away from us. My husband said, "What's he doing here?" We were excited as we hopped off the train to see him, but when we turned back to greet him he was gone—just disappeared!

We had the strangest feeling about it and agreed we would call them when we returned home. We found out later that Bill had pancreatic cancer, and he passed away only five months after our trip. Who then was the identical twin we saw at the little train station ...or was it just our imagination?

My husband's sister, Dana, told us that, before Bill died, he looked exactly like his deceased father because of all his weight loss. We also learned that Bill's family was from the Netherlands! Could what we saw have been an apparition of Bill's father? We now think so. We feel that this clairvoyant sighting of Bill's father was a sign that Bill's departed family was preparing to meet him on the other side, and what an appropriate setting—the train station, representing travel from "one side to the other."

The Victorian Lady
by Connie C.

One summer afternoon several years ago, my aunt saw a vision of an elegant lady in a large plumed hat and a Victorian-era dress walking through her living room. She wondered what this "spirit" was doing in her house, so she followed. Soon, the lady walked toward the front door and then disappeared right through it!

As my aunt opened the door and looked out into the street, what she saw stunned her. A little boy had been hit by a car and thrown from his bike! He was lying in a pool of blood right in front of the house, but he was still alive and desperately needed help. She immediately ran back into the house and dialed "911." Soon, the ambulance came, and she rode with the boy to the hospital. Later, they were able to identify the boy and call his parents, who rushed to his side.

My aunt kept in close touch with the boy's parents during his recovery, which resulted in a growing friendship between them. When he was able to return to school, they invited her to dinner at their home to celebrate. As she walked into their living room, she gasped! Hanging above an old chest of drawers was a portrait of the very same Victorian lady my aunt had seen walking through her home the afternoon the boy was hurt. When she inquired, she found out the lady was the boy's great-grandmother! She then felt compelled to tell his parents the whole story of how she had followed the lady spirit outside that day and was ultimately led to their son. His parents became teary eyed as they said that somehow they knew a higher power had sent a relative as a "guardian angel" (actually a "spirit guide") to save their boy's life. They were so grateful, at last, to know who it was!

Aunt Ruth's Request
by Marianne P.

In August of 1959, when I was 9 years old, my Aunt Ruth died, leaving behind four children—two of them were 1-year-old twins. Shortly after her death, I was awakened out of a sound sleep by a female voice calling my name. I got out of bed, turned on the bedside lamp, and went into the hallway to look around. I still heard my name being called, so I walked through the hallway to my parent's bedroom. Their front window was open, and that's where the voice seemed to be coming from. When I looked out, Aunt Ruthie was standing on the lawn in front of the house. The moonlight was bright, and I could plainly see the blue and red flower print of her dress! I called down to her, and she looked up, waved, and asked me to help look after the twins, and I said, "OK." Then, my dad woke up and wanted to know what I was doing and who I was shouting to. When I told him, he said it was just a dream and to go back to bed. I did go back to bed, but I was wide awake and *knew* it was more than a dream. To this day, I can still see the whole thing in my mind, just as clear today as when it happened, and I have honored Aunt Ruth's request!

Paving the Pathway
by Holly L.

Even though it was difficult for me, I regularly visited my elderly great-aunt, who was staying in a nursing home when she was suffering with Alzheimer's disease. She was in the last stages of the disease, and she didn't even know I was there. She just sat there and stared off into space.

However, during one of my visits, something very moving happened. As I was sitting next to her, holding her hand, I glanced over to the corner of the room. There I saw two cloud-like presences floating about four feet off the floor! To me, they *felt* like two female energies. I was transfixed—I couldn't look away!

Suddenly, my great-aunt (who rarely spoke) looked in the direction of the corner and opened her mouth to say, "Hello Margaret and Sarah." These were the names of her mother and sister. I didn't move and just stared in amazement. I sat for about five minutes listening to my great-aunt having a conversation with Margaret and Sarah! She seemed happy and was more lucid than I'd seen or heard her for a long time. Finally, I too smiled and said "hello" to them. Then, they disappeared.

A few minutes later, I kissed my great-aunt on the forehead and said I'd return in a couple days. Two days later, however, my great-aunt passed away. I believe her mother and sister had come for her to "pave the pathway" to the other side. I felt privileged because I too had witnessed their coming. This has helped me feel quite differently about death and dying. If indeed we are met by those we've known and loved and lost, it will be so much easier to make the transition to the other side. It definitely gives me great comfort knowing my great-aunt is now happy and peaceful with her mother and sister.

Seeing Spirits
by Sally T.

While she was alive, my mother actually *saw* spirits. She said they were translucent, and she could see right through them. When Mother was a teenager, she and my grandmother were watching an old hotel being torn down in Wilmington, Delaware. The hotel had been in our family for many years and was the property of Mother's great-great-grandparents.

As one wall crashed down, an exposed stairway could be seen. My mother saw two figures from the spirit world in detail. She told Grammy that she saw a woman, dressed in black and wearing a brooch, standing at the top of the stairs. A man was on the next step down, wearing pants with suspenders and a white shirt. They stared directly at my mother, which really made an impact on her.

Later, when looking through some family photos from the turn of the century, we found a photo of my great-great-grandmother, Anne Gibson, and her husband, John, who had owned the hotel. Mother confirmed that they were the same people she saw on the steps that day the hotel was demolished.

Before my mother passed away, she and my father were in a nursing home. My dad was confined to a wheelchair, and he died first. My mother said she saw my father coming for her and knew it was "her time to go." Dad appeared in front of her wearing his favorite shirt and looking younger and stronger, and he was without the wheelchair. He was hovering slightly above her, and he projected only from his knees up.

Mother said it gave her great peace to see Dad waiting for her. She passed away a week later. Because of these encounters, I'm hopeful that they'll be waiting for me when it's my turn to cross over. In fact, I have no doubt that they will.

Jimmy's Unexpected Visit
by Peg O.

Jimmy was a couple of years older than me, and he was the best brother anyone could ask for. He was a funny, humble, and very sincere person, and he was also my best friend. Jimmy was sickly from the time he was 3 years old. He was diagnosed at a young age as a severe diabetic, and we almost lost him several times.

Against the odds, he married in his 20s and had four wonderful children. By the time he was only 35, Jimmy was totally blind, on kidney dialysis, and completely bedridden. But his sense of humor and the light of his soul still shone through. I would visit him faithfully once a week; we'd reminisce about our childhood together, and I'd read to him. These visits were very special for both of us.

Jimmy passed away when he was 40, leaving behind many people who loved and missed him. I felt guilty because I was healthy my whole life, and I wanted so much for him to be happy and free of illness. One night about a week after Jimmy died, I felt terribly sad and helpless, and I locked myself in the bathroom. I cried for hours. I was so exhausted I stumbled to bed and immediately fell asleep.

A short time later, I was awakened by a very brilliant, burning light. As I sat up in bed, I saw a ball of bright white light come through the blinds and land on the foot of my bed. Within seconds, the ball of light began to transform, and I could see that it was my brother Jimmy! I couldn't talk or move—I just stared at him. He looked so handsome and healthy, and he was lying there in a relaxed position with his hands behind his head and his legs casually crossed.

Jimmy had a youthful attitude and smiled at me. He telepathically communicated with me for a long time and frequently laughed. For the life of me, I don't remember what he said, but I do remember him saying at the end, "Gotta go now." I pleaded with him to stay, but he said in a peppy, matter-of-fact way, "Peg, I *have* to." And then his body changed back into the glowing ball of brilliant light, went up through the blinds, and flew out the window!

I shot straight out of bed and ran to the blinds to see if the light burned them, but, of course, there was no burn mark. The whole experience left me awestruck but content. Jimmy had visited me that night to ease my pain and to let me know he was happy and at peace in the light. It was the greatest gift I could have received during a time of tremendous grief. And, I will always be thankful for it.

Luminous Beings
by Jim G.

In my late teens and into my 20s, strange occurrences began happening when I was asleep at night. I would sit up in bed and become conscious that something had just arrived in my bedroom. Then, I'd see luminous beings that took the form of light blue spheres. A surge of energy would go through my body, and the entire room would be filled with an intense blue light.

Many times during these visits, two huge figures would emerge, seated in a lotus position. They would silently hover at the foot of my bed. They did not appear to be angels. Instead, to me, they looked very much like Buddhist monk-type figures.

This occurred for years, until one night I said, "Who are you and why are you here?" Just then, the two spheres of light floated over to my head region—one on my left side and the other on my right. A deep male voice then said, "Don't be afraid—we are your guides!" After that, a female voice said, "We wish you no harm, only that love and peace will remain with you always."

Today, I can still shut my eyes and see their warm blue light within me. In addition, ever since that night, my senses have been heightened! Now, if I am near a spiritual place—like a church or a temple—I can see auras of different-colored light around other people. My guides' gift of insight has helped me with discernment throughout my lifetime, and for this I am forever grateful.

Birthday Surprise
by Mari D.

My dad was my best friend, and I loved him dearly. After he passed away, I read a lot of books about healing and began a spiritual journey. The feeling of his "presence" in spirit has helped me bring closure around his death.

In the fall of 2003, I was visiting with some very close friends for a few days. They have a beautiful bicentennial home in the country, which is perfectly restored. My dad considered them part of our family, since we spent a lot of time together and got to know each other well when I was growing up.

My favorite room in my friends' home is the parlor. It's filled with many antiques and has a wonderful, large fireplace with a gilt gold-framed mirror hanging above it. While I was visiting, my friends had a small get-together at their home on October 23rd, which just happened to be my dad's birthday. We gathered in the parlor for drinks, laughter, and good conversation. I couldn't resist taking pictures of everyone having fun.

I specifically took a picture of the crackling fire, the mantle strewn with candles, and the antique mirror. When I got home, I had the pictures developed. As I looked through them, one picture in particular grabbed my attention. It was the one I took of the fireplace. When I looked closely at it, I noticed something amazing—my dad's face was reflected in the mirror above the mantle!

He had a slight smile on his face and looked quite pleasant and happy. I sent copies to my friends, and they couldn't believe what they saw. It was as if my dad was joining in on the fun that night of his birthday, sending his love and his caring presence to everyone there.

Uncle Albert's Good-bye
by Anne F.

When I was 12 years old, my mother's younger brother Albert was my godfather and my favorite uncle. Uncle Albert was always at our house visiting, and I adored him.

I used to sleep in a king-sized canopy bed with my 16-year-old sister. One night, she woke me with the covers pulled over her head and shakily whispered, "There's somebody in the room." I wasn't at all afraid, so I sat up in bed and looked around. I saw a shape that looked like Uncle Albert standing at the foot of the bed and said to my sister, "Go back to sleep. It's only Uncle Albert." I looked over at the digital clock and noticed the time was 4:05 a.m.

The next morning was Sunday, and my parents weren't in the house, which we both thought was odd. We assumed they were at church, so we got dressed and went over to church ourselves. To our surprise, our parents weren't at church either. When we arrived home, they were sitting in the living room with pale looks on their faces. My mother had been crying. She announced that Uncle Albert had had an unexpected heart attack the night before and died in his sleep. The time was around 4 a.m.!

I believe that Uncle Albert appeared to say good-bye to me, and that has always given me a lot of comfort. I loved him dearly, and I know his love will always be with me.

David Leads the Way
by Cathy M.

My brother David and my mother were very close. Even though Mother tried not to show partiality, we knew David was her favorite. He would come home late many nights, and my mother would always lie awake and wait for him to pass her open bedroom door on the way to his room, which was right next to hers. One night, when David was just 19, he didn't come home. He was killed tragically that night in a car accident. For a long time after David's death, my mother would lie awake staring at her open bedroom door, as if she was wishing he'd pass by one last time.

Ten years later, my mother was diagnosed with lung cancer. She tried very hard to fight it, but, after the doctor removed one lung, it spread to the other. One January day, which happened to be my niece Jessi's birthday, my mother was told she had just a couple of days to live. We all stayed at her hospital bedside that night—my dad, my sister, my older brother, and me. I told them I knew she wouldn't pass away that night because it was Jessi's birthday, and Jessi was my mother's favorite niece.

My dad and brother were sitting on chairs beside Mother's bed, while my sister and I were kneeling on the floor. It was just before midnight when we heard footsteps coming down the hall. We all assumed the person was a nurse or an intern. However, when we glanced at the stranger passing by Mother's open door, we were speechless. It was my brother David!

He was wearing jeans and the same shirt he'd worn the night he was killed. He looked in at my mother, smiled, and then kept walking down the hall. We all sat frozen in time—like we were in a surreal world you read about but never actually experience. Finally,

I spoke up and said, "Did you see David?" Everyone in the room nodded yes. As we spoke about it, we all agreed: David had come to take my mother home to Heaven with him. We were absolutely sure it was David because he passed her hospital room door and walked down the hall, just as she'd wished he would do all those nights, 10 years before.

Two hours later, which was the day after Jessi's birthday, my mother went to Heaven. After the funeral, we told the rest of the family what we'd seen at the hospital, but they thought we were crazy. The pastor of our church, however, told them that, indeed, sometimes God does send messengers to guide loved ones home.

To this day, the memory of this experience gives me chills. However, it also brings me peace. I now tell others that it's OK to let go of loved ones who are dying because God will send a messenger who they love to take them on the journey back home. And I know that now, once again, my mother and David are together.

The Duke of Earl
by Helen D.

My grandfather died about 20 years ago, but he's come back to visit me several times since then. One of those visits happened in the fall of 2002 when my husband and I were on a cruise. One night at dinner, I glanced to the end of the table of 12 people and saw a gentleman who looked exactly like my grandfather. He was wearing the same style navy-blue suit and cufflinks my grandpa always wore, and he had the same mannerisms as well!

After dinner, the man walked over to me and introduced me to his companion. She was an Irish woman named Mary. My grandmother was also Irish and named Mary, which I thought was strange. He said to me, "You have a beautiful smile, so don't ever stop smiling!" No one had ever said that to me ...except my dear grandpa!

I didn't get the strange man's name that night. However, a couple of nights later, he sat at our table again. My grandfather's name was Charles, but everyone called him "Earl" or, jokingly, the "Duke of Earl." When I finally asked the stranger his name, it turned out to be Earl!

After dinner, we stopped by the library to look at the answers from a quiz given onboard ship the day before. The first question was "A name that means royalty," and the two answers were "Duke" or "Earl." Now, this was really becoming like the "Twilight Zone"! My husband agreed that it was very weird.

We didn't see Earl or his companion Mary again until we were disembarking from the ship. I was standing in the lobby, and Earl walked across the room, grabbed my arm and said, "Until we meet again." Well, I almost fell over! That was my grandfather's favorite song, and he had requested that it be played at his funeral. I couldn't speak for a few minutes, and, just like that, Earl disappeared into the crowd.

Another incident happened in June, 2003, when I was at a rehearsal dinner for my best friend's wedding. Across the room was an older gentleman who again looked like my grandpa. He walked over and touched my arm and said I had a beautiful smile and not to lose it. When I asked my girlfriend who he was, she said he was an acquaintance of her fiancé's best friend, and his name was Duke!

I truly believe my grandpa overshadowed both these men to reach out and communicate with me.

Great-Grandma Baby-sits
by Patty C.

When I was only 19 and first married, my husband and I and our infant son Steven lived in a duplex. The bedrooms were on the second floor. One day, while my son took his nap, I went out back to hang clothes on the line. I saw some movement out of the corner of my eye and happened to glance up to the second-story window of Steven's room. There was a woman standing at the window! She wore a black dress, had her hair neatly arranged in a bun, and was looking down at me.

I raced into the house and up the stairs to Steven's room, taking the steps two at a time. When I got to his room, there was no one there …only Steven, sleeping peacefully in his crib. I thought at first that someone was trying to abduct my little boy. But my landlord, Mr. Holt, assured me that he had neither heard nor seen anyone come in the front door. I thought I was losing my mind until I mentioned the incident to my mother. She smiled and said not to worry; it was probably an angel watching over my baby.

Six years later, I finally found out who the mysterious woman was. At that time, one of my aunts gave me a picture of my great-grandmother, and I had the tiny photo enlarged as a gift for my mother. I noticed immediately that the woman in the photo was the same woman I'd seen in the window of Steven's room that day. She wore the same dark dress, and her hair was in the same neat bun. And, of course, I could *never* forget her face.

It was true: my great-grandma was watching over my infant son, and, I guess, was protecting me too. When I gave the picture to my mother, she wept. I reminded her of the strange woman in the window six years before and asked if she thought it was great-grandma. She said she was sure it was—her grandmother loved babies.

Since that time, I've seen other souls in my home, and I'm always able to discover who they are by seeing old family photos. It seems many of my ancestors are available to watch over me and my family! Love never dies, and it's reassuring to know they're still with us and protecting us.

An Apparition of Healing
by Brenda Z.

It's been 14 years since my brother's death, but the events surrounding his passing are as vivid in my memory as if they happened yesterday. I had fallen asleep on my couch, and at about 12:20 a.m. awoke in a state of panic, with my heart pounding and my thoughts racing. An hour later, I found out why.

After a long bout with depression and drug abuse, my brother had succumbed to committing suicide. His death troubled me for months. I felt tremendous guilt and anger about it, making it very hard for me to get on with my life.

A few months later, I was asleep in bed and had an "out-of-body" experience in which I was floating on top of the ceiling, looking down at my body below. I saw my husband sleeping beside me and noticed that my 2-year-old son had crawled in between us.

He looked so precious and small lying there. It gave me a quiet, calm, peaceful feeling watching this scene from above.

I noticed every tiny detail in the moonlit bedroom—my digital clock glowing on my nightstand, my hair brush lying on the dresser, and my pink robe hanging over the chair—all from an aerial perspective. Just then, as I looked out the bedroom window, my brother appeared! He had the biggest smile on his face, and he held out his hand to me. I calmly said to him, "How are ya?" And we telepathically had what seemed to be a long conversation. Memories of our childhood together and events we experienced flashed through my mind, and my brother seemed happy and animated as he sent me messages.

The next morning, I felt wonderful! I didn't recall any of the conversation with my brother from the night before—all I knew was the guilt and anger I had harbored for so long was now gone! I felt totally renewed.

To this day my brother still comes around. Every now and then, we'll hear a special knock on our bedroom door that we know is him. But I'll never forget that most powerful visit from him. It convinced *me* that the soul is eternal and that I'm never alone.

One Last Good-bye
by Judy A.

Six weeks after my brother died, we went to the cemetery to lay his gravestone. I had my trusty Polaroid camera along to take pictures of his grave and the lovely pond behind it. The camera was a few years old and always took great pictures. After the rest of our group went back to the car, I stayed behind to snap pictures.

I waited for the photos to develop and then put them in my coat pocket without looking at them, because it was a very cold day. A few hours later, someone reminded me to remove the photos from my pocket and share them. As we looked at them, we all noticed something very strange on the last picture taken: there was a large gray mist over my brother's grave and in the mist a face that looked like …my brother!

It really surprised and scared us because the other pictures were normal. The eerie mist of the apparition never happened before or since that day in any of my pictures at the cemetery. We all believe it was my brother miraculously appearing. It looked and *felt* like his energy on that photo. We agreed that it must have been his way of saying one last good-bye.

Chapter Four

Clairaudience (Hearing)

"What the dead had no speech for, when living, they can tell you, being dead: the communication
of the dead is tongued with the fire beyond the language of the living."
– George Eliot

Clairaudience means "clear hearing." Everyone at one time or another has *heard* a "voice" inside their head, directing them or commenting on their actions. Sometimes, though, the voice is more distinct or direct. Loved ones who have crossed can communicate *telepathically* by planting impressions in our minds. For example, I've heard my mother Dorothy call out to me upon awakening. I've also heard my male guardian angel speak to me many times. Departed loved ones can also communicate through a song on the radio or even through telephone lines. The following are a few experiences I've had with clairaudience, followed by stories from friends and clients.

Do Not Take Anything for Granted

One morning, I woke up and heard a deep male voice say very plainly, "Do not take anything for granted." As I pondered what that meant, I had a feeling it would be "one of those days"! At my art gallery, I arranged my display screens by the back door so my business partner could load them into the van. We then went to lunch, and when we returned, all 12 large display screens were gone! We panicked because the art show was the next day in another state.

We called the manufacturer (who luckily happened to be just a few miles from us), and they supplied us with a new set "on loan," of course. We learned later that one of the renters in my building thought the screens were being thrown out, so he packed them in his van and took them home. Later, he apologized and returned them to us. In essence, my angel was warning me to be careful and not to take anything for granted. I certainly learned my lesson and decided that, whenever I heard the deep male voice again, I would listen!

You Have a Great Smile

It wasn't long after that that I did indeed hear that voice again. This is another amazing story of how I met my wonderful husband Jon. I had been divorced for 16 years and had dated men from all walks of life. I knew in my heart that there was someone out there for me, but we just couldn't seem to connect. One night, I had a dream, where I heard angels' voices say, "Make a list—make a list for a man!" I had never thought about it that way before, but *thought plus energy does equal form*; and we are all the product of our thinking. The Universe is simple—what we program in through our thought processes is returned to us.

So, I sat down and made my list. I simply wrote, "Dear Lord, I am ready to attract my true soul mate, companion, and husband for both our highest good. I want him to be eligible and willing to commit." Then I wrote down five qualities that I wanted in another human being. No one is perfect, so I figured that a list of a few qualities was a good starting place. I made two copies of the list— putting one on the nightstand next to my bed and the other in my purse. Every couple of days, I prayed over the lists, saying I was ready for the man to come into my life.

Three months later, on Valentine's Day, I was out with a group of people. There were about 200 others at the event we attended. I was on my way to the ladies room, purse in hand, with my list in my purse. I glanced across the room and in the corner stood a tall handsome gentleman. Just then, I heard that deep male voice whisper in my ear, "That's the man you're going to marry!" I thought I was hearing things, so I continued on to the rest room. But again, and even louder this time, the voice repeated, *"That's the man you're going to marry!"*

I felt paralyzed—I couldn't move forward. So, I turned around and slowly started walking towards the attractive man in the corner. Thoughts flashed through my mind: What am I going to say? What if he's married? By that time, I was standing in front of him, and I heard myself blurt out, "Who's your dentist? You have a great smile!" I was embarrassed, but he just stood there beaming. He took my hand, introduced himself, and history was made. Jon proposed exactly two years later—on Valentine's Day—and, of course, I accepted. He possessed all the qualities on my list, but it was my angel's insistent voice that first propelled me to his side.

It's important to listen to promptings from spirit. These voices are not your imagination. They are loving guides and angels trying to help, if only you'll open your heart and mind to listen.

Clair de Lune

Songs can also be a form of clairaudience or *clear hearing*—a very direct way a soul can communicate with us. For example, my mother Dorothy loved the French song "Clair de Lune" written by Debussy. She would play it for me on the piano, and, we played it, on her request, at her funeral. I later built a "memorial" music room in our home in Dorothy's honor. It contains a beautiful antique piano and several music boxes—many of which play "Clair de Lune."

One morning, I awoke to music playing and heard strains of "Clair de Lune" wafting up to my bedroom from the downstairs music room. Upon investigation, I found that three of her music boxes were playing simultaneously! It was her way of saying "Good morning!" From then on, I heard "Clair de Lune" wherever I went—in the mall, at a restaurant, even in a doctor's office. It's not a common piece of music to hear, but this went on for a couple of months …and then it ceased. I knew that Dorothy was around me when I heard her song, and it was a very direct way for her to tell me that she loved me. Now, when I hear "Clair de Lune," I know that my mother is saying "hello."

What a Wonderful World
By Dale C.

My best friend Koren was only 26 years old when she learned she had melanoma. It was the aggressive kind, and she was told she had only four months to live. She went home from the hospital to spend her remaining days with her precious 5-year-old daughter, Tyler.

Koren made me promise I'd be a good godmother, after she departed, and take good care of Tyler. It was very difficult watching her deteriorate, but all the while her attitude was very positive and optimistic. When she felt depressed, she would play Louis Armstrong's song, "What a Wonderful World." It was uplifting for her to listen to, as she counted her blessings.

One day when I was visiting, she said, "Now, Dale, I don't have long to live; and I want you somehow to have this song sung at my funeral. I want people to be happy for me because I'm going to a better place, and I want them to count their blessings." And I promised I would.

One Thursday morning, soon after, I received a phone call from Koren's mother saying Koren had died at home during the night, with her little girl Tyler by her side. Everyone was confused—even though they knew her death was imminent, they were still shocked. She and her family had decided that cremation would be best, along with a simple memorial service.

There was a lot of hurrying and scurrying trying to make just the right funeral arrangements. I tried to remember Koren's last requests, but my mind was foggy. Then, it came to me—the song! But what was the name of the song? I couldn't remember. I asked her family to look through her things to see if they could find a record or CD by Louis Armstrong. But that was the least of their worries. They had no time to do it. So, in a state of panic, I said a prayer, "Koren, help me remember your song."

The next afternoon, I went to the florist to have a special arrangement made for her funeral—lilies were her favorite flower. I was driving back home and happened to turn on the car radio. All of a sudden, a familiar voice sang, "I see skies of blue, clouds of white, the bright blessed day, and the dark sacred night …and I think to myself, 'What a wonderful world.'" It was Koren's song! I immediately pulled over, grabbed a pen, and wrote down the lyrics.

At Koren's funeral, a very accomplished tenor sang, "What a Wonderful World," and we all could feel her beautiful spirit, as we listened and wept …and only *I* knew that it was Koren, herself, that played the song on the car radio to help me remember.

Note from Michele: *Dale Carroll, who submitted this story in December 2003, was one of my first and very dearest clients. She was truly an "earth angel", with a sweet and kind demeanor. Dale passed away from cancer on May 10, 2004 (the day after Mother's Day). She left behind a beautiful 15-year-old daughter, Lindsay, who I promised to mentor. She also was a glowing example of God's grace while here on Earth and will always have a very special place in my heart. She acted as a "bridge" between dimensions and helped many souls to make transition to the other side as a hospice volunteer. She was also a gifted pianist and composer.*

A Collect Call from Heaven
by Lisa J.

My good friend Patti and her dad Bill were the best of friends. They didn't act like your typical father and daughter, but more like buddies. Bill was quite a character, and he loved to visit the casinos in Atlantic City a couple times a month to try his luck.

When Patti became an adult, she'd accompany her dad on his casino trips. They always had such fun, and she told me she had many fond memories of those trips. They were very good times!

Tragically, Bill was diagnosed with cancer in October, 2001, and died just three months later, right before Christmas. Patti was terribly heartbroken. Not only did she miss her dad a lot, but she wasn't there when he died, and in her mind, they never really had a chance to say good-bye.

Patti asked her dad for a "sign" that he was OK on the other side, feeling that whatever way he chose to communicate would be unique, because that's the kind of person he was.

A few months passed without any sign from her dad. Then, one night, Patti was awakened by the phone ringing at 2 a.m. It was someone calling from her dad's favorite casino in Atlantic City. The operator asked her if she'd accept a collect call from a man named Bill! When she accepted the call, she didn't hear a voice on the other end but instead felt a *presence*. Patti just *knew* it was her dad!

Afterwards, she felt comforted that he was thinking of her and wanted to tell her he was OK. Bill had called from Heaven to give Patti a *special* good-bye!

Voice of an Angel
by Lynn M.

Nineteen years ago, when my son was just 5, something amazing happened that he still talks about today. It was a stifling August afternoon, and we were driving to the garage to have my car's air conditioning unit fixed. Of course, we had the windows rolled down trying to get any waft of breeze we could.

As we drove along, I suddenly heard a voice say, "Roll up your son's window!" I thought it was weird and rationalized that the voice must be my imagination. However, a little farther down the road the voice repeated the message, this time a little louder—telling me to *"roll up the window."* Again, I ignored it.

Soon after, we were driving through a residential neighborhood, and I slowed down to stop at a red light. This time, the strange voice blared in my ear (as if the volume had been turned up 10 times), "ROLL UP YOUR SON'S WINDOW, NOW!"

Without hesitating, I leaned over my son and rolled up the passenger side window. I remember him saying, "Mommy, it's so hot. Please leave my window open." But, just then, we passed some workers who were mulching tree branches with a large wood chopper, and a huge chunk of a branch flew out of the chopper and slammed with great force into my son's closed window!

It cracked the glass, but miraculously, it didn't shatter it. We were both quite shocked and couldn't speak. But most of all, we were greatly relieved that at least my son wasn't hurt. When we finally got to the garage, the attendant checked the cracked window. He agreed that, if the window had been rolled down, my son could have been critically injured or perhaps even killed. I feel the voice that spoke to me that day was that of an angel, protecting him from harm. It taught me that God's grace is always with us, we just have to *listen*!

The Mysterious Voice
by Lynette S.

It was October 27—my son's third birthday. That morning, I drove him to daycare and then went on to work. I usually took the trolley because it stopped right outside my front door, but I needed the car that day to run errands after work and prepare for my son's birthday party.

The two of us lived in a large apartment complex, and each building in the complex contained two apartments. Another single mother had just moved into the apartment above us, and she and I rapidly became good friends. That day, I left work early—at 3 p.m.—to go to daycare and pick up my boy for his party. I quickly bought a gift and was on my way home to drop it off before meeting him and then going on to the supermarket.

While driving towards my apartment with the gift, I heard a voice telling me not to go home. It was a deep voice, and it rang loudly in my ears. For some reason, I felt compelled to listen to it. So I went on to the supermarket, where I bought a small cake for my son. The market was just across the street from my apartment at a large intersection. I thought, "It won't take too long to drop off the cake and gift," and I headed toward home. But, once again, the voice spoke, and this time it was even more emphatic. It said, "*Stop! Don't go home!*"

Automatically, I turned into a gas station and got out to pump some gas. By then, I was confused and irritated, but I still felt listening to the mysterious voice was the right thing to do. After I paid for the gas, the familiar voice called out once again, "Lynette, do *not* go home." So, I stopped and purchased Chinese food for dinner. Since time was ticking away, I realized that I needed to head straight over to pick up my son, without first emptying the car.

When I arrived at daycare, he was ecstatic to see me and ran into my arms. I was agitated for being slightly late and I apologized to his teacher. We then headed for home and finally arrived at the apartment. When I pulled into my parking place, the mysterious voice now said reassuringly, "OK. It's safe." But when I started to put my key in the front door, it swung open. All the lights were on inside, and there were papers strewn everywhere. My home was completely bare! It had been completely ransacked and vandalized! Appliances, televisions, stereo, jewelry—all gone!

My friend upstairs was also robbed. When the police arrived, it was determined that the break-in occurred between 3:00 and 4:30 p.m.—the exact time I was out doing errands! We found out later that the robbers were dangerous—armed men wanted for two bank robberies and thefts all over the state. They had been watching my neighbor and me because we were single parents, and they knew we usually didn't return home until 6 p.m.

If my son and I would have arrived home while the vandals were there, we could have been severely hurt or even killed. As I explained to the officers that "a voice" stalled me from coming home, I went into shock. It finally hit me: I realized my life and possibly my son's life had been saved that day by an unknown "helper." I will be forever grateful to that special someone (or *angel!*) who saved us from harm.

A Better Way Home
Anonymous

My husband passed away in April, 2003. For many years, while he was alive, we attended all the local hockey games in town. Seventy-two times a year we traveled the same road to and from the games, because we never had a reason to take another road.

Then, in February, 2004, I was on my way home from a game with my daughter in the car. We were, of course, taking the same road we always did. However, for some reason on that particular night, about midway through the ride home I heard a voice say to take a different route home. So, I turned onto another road from the main street, and, just as I made the turn onto the new street, a car went flying through the intersection where we would have been stopped, smashing into two other cars!

There's no doubt that the car my daughter and I were in would have been one of those two cars if I hadn't heard something inside tell me "to take another route" that night. If it hadn't been for that voice, my daughter and I could have been killed! I am sure that "voice" was my husband, and, because of him, my daughter and I were protected that night.

Dad Did It His Way
by Roseann B.

One night, I woke up abruptly from a dream. In the dream, my mom and dad were cleaning out his closet and getting rid of his clothes. Inside one of his suit pockets, my mom found a picture of the two of them. She asked my dad why she was standing in the foreground of the picture and why he was in the background. At that moment, the picture tore in half, leaving her holding only her image. Right after my dream, my mom called me to say my dad had just died of a heart attack.

That in itself was amazing; but after Dad's passing, he began communicating with us in many different ways, and one of them really stands out in my mind.

Two years after Dad died, my sister Francine, my cousin Terri, my friend Danny, and I were at a restaurant. On that particular night, there was a band playing that occasionally, right in the middle of a song, would break into something completely different—like the theme from "The Brady Bunch"! This added an element of surprise and variation to their music.

As we were eating and talking, they happened to break into the song, "My Way," by Frank Sinatra which caught our attention. That was my dad's favorite song! After the song ended, we noticed that my cousin, Terri, was crying. She wouldn't tell us why because she said, "You'll think I'm crazy!"

When we finally convinced her to tell us, she said that she saw my dad standing right next to her; and he said, "Tell my girls that I love them."

As we finished our dinner, we talked about what happened and tried to make sense of it, but we never came up with an answer. Then, at the end of the evening, we realized we had all had a few too many cocktails and did not have a designated driver. Since I only had two drinks, I volunteered to drive everyone home …but when I put my key into the car door, it immediately broke in half! I barely turned the key, but I felt as if it had become like a soft piece of clay. As a result, we had to wait for a cab to take us home. Later, we found out that there had been a major accident on our route home that we could have been in. We all truly believed Dad not only appeared and talked to us that night, but he was not going to let me drive because of potential danger. However, the most unbelievable part of the story is yet to come!

A couple weeks later, we all went back to hear the same band play; however when we requested that they play "My Way" again, to honor my dad, they told us that they have never, ever played that song! It had been Dad communicating with us in *his* own way that night to keep us out of harm's way!

A Surprise Call
by Joyce M.

My husband Dan was a wonderful man. I met him at Cape Cod one summer when I was in my late teens. I guess you could say it was love at first sight. We were young and impulsive, and we married the next summer. I worked to help put him through school, and he became a very successful engineer.

During our 32-year marriage, Dan and I raised three beautiful children—two sons and a daughter. He would call me from work at least once a day, just to say hello and ask me how my day was going. It may sound odd, but our marriage remained fresh and full of surprises all the years we were together.

One night around 3 a.m., I got up to go to the bathroom and came back to bed. As I lay down, it occurred to me that my husband wasn't snoring—and he was quite a snorer! I leaned over and gently put my hand on his shoulder. He didn't move. I softly called his name. He didn't respond. I turned on the lamp on my side of the bed and shook him. He was lifeless. The color was gone from his cheeks, and his hands were cold. In a panic, I called "911." Everything after that was a blur. Dan had died that night in his sleep of a massive heart attack.

It was a terrible shock to lose the love of my life so abruptly. My children were a big support, although my daughter was devastated because she was very close to her dad. The community rallied at Dan's funeral—there must have been at least 300 people in attendance. Everyone loved him. My son, Daniel, Jr., wrote and read something very special about his dad at the funeral, and there wasn't a dry eye at the service. My daughter Debra insisted on putting a family portrait in the coffin with her dad.

I prayed to Dan for a sign that he was all right, at peace, and in Heaven with our other loved ones, and I told my children about it. My son (our youngest) brought his cell phone to the memorial. At the last minute, he said, "Mom, Dad always called you every day, so I'm going to put the phone in the coffin too. Maybe he'll call you someday from the other side!" And with that he put the phone alongside Dan's body, but only the two of us knew.

For months after his passing, insomnia was a constant problem for me. I also cried every night, so my doctor put me on an antidepressant. Nothing in my life was the same without my dear husband. I prayed for peace, but I found none. Then, one night, exactly six months after Dan's death, something miraculous happened.

The phone on my nightstand rang at 3 a.m. I was confused and groggy, wondering if it was one of the children. I slowly answered, "Hello." There was a pause that seemed like an eternity. Then, I heard Dan's voice! It was clear and distinct. He said, "I'm fine, Joyce. I love you." And then there was silence.

The phone stayed in my hand for about five minutes. I couldn't believe what I'd heard. When the shock wore off, I hit "star 69" to get the phone number of the last caller. The recording said the number was "outside of the immediate dialing area..." That made perfect sense, since it was a call from Heaven! It was Dan ...I *felt* it, I *knew* it!

After that, my healing process began. I haven't shared this with many people, but I read somewhere that departed loved ones can communicate through phone lines. Well, it happened to me, and it's changed my perspective on the afterlife. The soul *is* eternal. It loves and remembers all. Dan surprised me with one last call, and that's all I needed to feel more at peace.

Ask and You Will Receive
by Lynne K.

My dad and I were very close. I was his only daughter and "Daddy's little girl," so to speak. The last time we were physically together was on the day of my wedding, when he proudly walked me down the aisle. When I returned from my honeymoon, I was told Dad had died instantly of a brain aneurism. It was a terrible shock, especially since the last time I saw him he was so full of joy.

Two weeks after Dad died, I was driving home from the store and thinking about him. I had the radio on and had read somewhere that spirits can communicate through the radio. So, I called out for Dad to contact me. Within seconds, a song by Luther Vandross came on the radio. It was called "If I Could Dance with My Father Again."

I immediately got the chills, and was so touched that I began to cry uncontrollably. The lyrics of the song seemed like they had been written just for me! And, the song had come on the radio just after I asked my dad to talk to me! I cried all the way home that day, but I now know that I can connect with my dad anytime I want. All I have to do is ask!

It's Time to Play the Guitar

The "spirit" or "soul" is electromagnetic energy. It can literally travel through electrical or phone lines to communicate with us, as in the story "A Surprise Call" by Joyce M. A few years ago, I had a remarkable experience with a soul who wanted to make his presence known, and I'd like to share it with you.

It started with my stepdaughter, Tina, giving me a CD of soothing classical guitar music. Her friend, Matthew, was the featured musician who composed the music and played his guitar on the CD. It was calming and meditative, and I often enjoyed listening to it before doing readings.

About two weeks later, I was conducting a phone reading for a lady in California from my office in Pennsylvania. I had the tape player on and was about halfway through the one-hour session, when all of a sudden, we both heard static. The static increased, and I called my client's name, but she didn't respond. Then, a distinct male voice came over the phone line and slowly mouthed the words, "Play the guitar. It's time to play the guitar." It seemed like it took a great deal of energy for him to say those words.

Then, the static stopped; and I heard the lady from California say to me, "Did you hear that?" Both of us were alone in our houses at the time, and we knew somehow the phone lines must have been overshadowed by someone else. It was an eerie feeling, but we laughed it off.

Something prompted me to make a copy of the tape of my reading with the lady (which had the interruption by the mysterious male voice on it) before sending the original to her. The haunting voice didn't leave my mind, so I tried to figure out what it meant.

A few minutes later, while I was praying for guidance, my stepdaughter called. I played the tape of the male voice talking about the guitar for her. She agreed that it was chilling and sounded "other-worldly." Then, out of nowhere, I heard myself saying to Tina, "Do you think it has to do with your friend Matthew?" She said she didn't know but would give him a call.

Matthew called me before nightfall, and I carefully explained what had happened that afternoon with the mysterious voice. He cautiously agreed to listen to the tape. Afterwards, he was silent.

Finally, I said, "Matthew, I'm sorry if this doesn't make sense to you." He hesitated and said, "That's unmistakably the voice of my friend Steve, who died in the mountains about a year ago!" Trying to piece things together, I asked Matthew why his friend would mention the guitar. In response, Matthew shared the following story:

His good friend Steve, whom he'd known since childhood, had disappeared in the woods last year. Steve had been dating a beautiful girl from New England who would drive to Pennsylvania for visits. One weekend, they had a fight, and Steve just disappeared. They racked their brains to figure out where he might have gone, and his girlfriend started to feel guilty about the whole thing. Matthew remembered that, when Steve was upset, he would walk in the dense mountain woods in northern Pennsylvania.

One day blurred into the next, and three months had gone by since Steve had been seen. Finally, the police found Steve's body 20 miles north of his usual walking trail. The cause of death was unknown. His family absolutely couldn't figure out how he got lost, since he knew the trail by heart. Steve was an insulin-dependent diabetic who always carried insulin with him. He never would have wandered off so far by himself without it.

Matthew also told me he'd had a visit from Steve's girlfriend a few days before, and she was leaving that night. He mentioned the tape I had and suggested that she listen to it, so hopefully, she could get some peace by hearing Steve's voice one last time.

Later, I called her and played the tape. She cried a long time and then said she was grateful that her boyfriend made an attempt to communicate. She also mentioned something astounding. She and Steve both loved a jazz song entitled "It's Time to Play the Guitar," and they had listened to it together the night before he disappeared. Steve had used the title of this song as one last communication from the other side to his best friend and girlfriend through a chance encounter on the phone. This experience was a confirmation for me that souls still care deeply for those left behind and will do anything they can to make a connection with those they love.

Chapter Five

Clairsentience (Feeling)

"Some feelings are to mortals given
With less of Earth in them than Heaven." – Sir Walter Scott

We've all experienced times when we had a *feeling* about something. Sometimes, we act upon these promptings, and sometimes we don't. It can be as simple as a strong urge to call a friend and then finding out, when we do, that he or she was just picking up the phone to call us …or had been thinking of us. Or, perhaps we've been driving home from work and had a *prompting* not to take the normal route …and then found out later that there'd been a major accident on our usual route, and we just missed being involved in it.

Clairsentience means "clear feeling," and we all have experienced it. Many times, angels and departed loved ones will *touch* us with their energy. We might feel a brush on our cheek, invisible hands on our shoulders, or a sensation of warmth or chills. Sometimes, it's just a comfortable, peaceful sensation from head to toe, and other times the feeling is very physical. I would like to start this chapter with the first *physical* touch I can remember receiving from an angel:

Touched from Beyond

In 1971, when I was attending college as an art education major, I was taking a wonderfully advanced jewelry-making class that everyone loved. The class was frequently engaged in cutting pieces of metal with precision saws, using blowtorches to solder the metal, and operating heavy jewelry-buffing machinery. We were told we had to focus our attention on what we were doing at all times.

One important rule that was always overlooked was to wear protective goggles and tie back our hair. At that time, I had waist-length hair that I wore loose and straight. The jewelry-buffing wheel was very large and had a very sharp edge. You could adjust the speed of the rotation by using pedals underneath the machine.

During class one gray winter afternoon, my mind was elsewhere and not on the task at hand. I hadn't remembered to tie my hair back or put on the protective goggles before I began using the buffing wheel. Suddenly, within a split second, my hair became entangled in the wheel, which rapidly pulled my face and eyes towards its sharp edge. My eyes were thrust within a millimeter of the rotating blade when I felt huge hands on both my shoulders. I was yanked backwards and catapulted to safety on the floor!

Everyone in class—including the professor—was screaming. In the moving wheel, I saw blood, a piece of my scalp, and lots of hair! It was a horrible sight! Miraculously, my face and eyes were totally unharmed. I received a good reprimand and many stitches.

Later, when I asked who had pulled me from harm, several classmates said they saw some invisible *force* pull me rapidly away from danger. All agreed they had never seen anything like it before. I now realize that that force was my guardian angel throwing me back out of harm's way. After that event, the rules in class were rigidly enforced, which probably saved many other students from a fate worse than mine.

Stop the Car
by Francis P.

My friend and I were driving to our high school reunion. We were very excited and chatted about who might be there and whether we thought they might have changed in some way. The reunion was being held at a very upscale resort located in the woods about an hour's drive from our home. I visited there several times when I was growing up but hadn't been there in years. I sort of remembered the directions and knew to turn left at the "Y" intersection.

As I approached this particular Y, a fog or confusion came over me. I just couldn't think, and I had a very strong *feeling* to stop the car! I immediately slammed on the brakes and stopped about 25 feet from the turn. Suddenly, a truck loaded with furniture came into the intersection. Then, a car came shooting out of the intersection and slammed into the side of the truck. My friend and I sat in amazement as we watched everything happening before us in "slow motion."

One by one, each piece of furniture spiraled out of the truck. People were thrown forward in their vehicles. It was a devastating accident. If I hadn't immediately stopped the car when I did, my friend and I would have been wedged in between the truck and the other car and possibly killed. It was as if time "stood still" or slowed down significantly for us. We thanked God for my "feeling" and still talk about that surreal incident today.

My Husband's Touch
by Kathryn M.

I married the love of my life and my best friend. We were very happy and very much in love. Throughout our marriage, whenever I was upset, my husband would always put his strong, warm hands on my shoulders. This seemed to calm me. It was his way of being there for me.

I lost him to a brain tumor when he was just 37—only three months before my son's first penance in church. Before going to church on the day of my son's first confession, I remember feeling fairly composed and strong. But, when I entered the church, grief overwhelmed me—an upsurge of anxiety I hadn't expected. I felt so sad that my husband was missing this important event in our son's life. I also felt bad that I was experiencing this event without him.

It was a cold winter day, but inside the church it was warm, with soft lighting and beautiful music playing in the background. The children went to the front of the church where they met the priests who were hearing their first confessions at the altar. I took a seat by myself in the last row and soon broke down into tears.

Suddenly, I felt two very strong, warm hands on my shoulders! I was so stunned that I sat perfectly still and was almost afraid to turn around. The pressure of the hands grew stronger. I knew there wasn't anyone sitting behind me, but I turned around anyway. I saw no one there.

The feeling of the hands eventually subsided, but the experience left me wide-eyed, surprised, and very comforted. My husband's special touch always calmed me down. And I know now that he realized I especially needed his touch that day.

An Unexpected Premonition
by Eileen E.

I have been an intensive care nurse for many years at a local hospital. One night while I was working, I was walking down the main corridor on my floor around 10 p.m., when thoughts of my ex-husband just popped into my head out of the blue. We had been estranged for a long time, so it surprised me that I would think of him. It was also interesting that at the time these thoughts came to me, I was holding a padded tongue blade that we use for patients who are having a seizure ...even though no one on the floor was having a seizure that evening. I felt rather strange and had chills from head to toe.

Then, a couple of days later, the man I was dating asked me if I had changed my last name back to my maiden name. I told him I hadn't. He then asked me my ex-husband's first name, which I thought was odd. When I told him, he handed me the obituary section of the newspaper. The first person listed there was my ex-husband! I was stunned and shocked and didn't know what to say.

Later, I contacted my ex-husband's family, and they verified that indeed he had passed away suddenly from some sort of seizure. The time of death was 9:58 p.m.—on the very same night that I had been thinking of him *and* holding a tongue blade for seizures! I thought to myself, "What are the chances of that?"

Even more interesting was the fact that my oldest daughter felt a draft in her bedroom that same night and thought immediately of her dad (my ex-husband) for some reason. I believe now that he had tried to communicate with both of us as he crossed over that night. I am grateful for that, because, since we were out of touch, I might never have found out he had died if he hadn't communicated with me and my daughter as he was "going home."

Hello from Steve
by Sherrie L.

My husband had a son, Steve, from a previous marriage whom he loved very much. Steve had a mischievous streak in him and a mind of his own. But we were totally shocked when Steve died from a drug overdose a couple of years ago. We were trying to help each other get through the grief and pain of it all.

In the funeral home, I was sitting alone a few rows behind my husband and didn't notice anyone around me. Our daughter was standing in front of the room, facing me, while reciting a tribute that she wrote about Steve. Suddenly, there was a hard tug on my ponytail! I turned around, but there was nobody behind me. I passed it off as my imagination.

A few minutes later, I felt the tug again. Still, there was no one behind me.

After the funeral, I mentioned my experience to my daughter, and she said she kept seeing me turn around and wondered why I was doing that. I told her someone was pulling on my hair! We're convinced it was my stepson, Steve, saying "hello" in his playful, mischievous way.

My daughter said, "Mom, he's probably telling you to let your hair down and relax, and not feel guilty about his death. He's in a better place now!" The more I thought about it, the more sure I was that she was right. Steve was a free spirit who wanted us to feel free too. What a comfort it was to know that.

Trust Your Feelings
by Lynn Y.

From the time I was a little girl, I could *feel* "energy" around me. I could also *feel* things that other people were feeling. And, whenever someone died, I'd briefly feel both chills and some of the symptoms that person had experienced with his or her illness. I read a book about people like me, and we are called "empaths"…born with an ability to empathically feel the feelings of other people.

An example of this happened a few years ago when we found out that my grandfather had a brain tumor. My family and I spent a lot of time with him in his last days while he was in a coma. One day, I was walking down the hall at school and suddenly felt ice-cold from my hands to my feet. My head started to pound and ache terribly, and I felt very dizzy. I looked over at my friend, who was walking with me, and said, "Grandpa just died." She said, "No, don't worry. He's fine."

Ten minutes later, I was called to the principal's office, where I found my mom crying hysterically. My grandfather had just passed away from his brain tumor, which had hemorrhaged. I told my mom about the pain I had experienced minutes earlier, and we figured out that my grandfather had died at exactly the same time I felt the symptoms of his hemorrhage.

About a week later, a similar incident happened. I felt pain in my left arm (as if it was paralyzed), tremendous pressure on my chest, and my body turned ice-cold. Soon after, I learned that my good friend's grandfather had died of a heart attack at the same time I felt that pain. I now share these empathic experiences with others to enlighten them and let them know that you *can* trust your feelings!

Chapter Six

Olfactory Occurrences (Smelling)

"Only the actions of the just smell sweet and blossom in their dust."
– James Shirley

Many people at my seminars ask about the sense of smell: "Could I possibly smell my dad's cigarette smoke after he passed away or the fragrance of my grandmother's flowers in my room?" The answer is yes; spirit can formulate smells, smoke, and fragrances for you. It's one of the rarest forms of communication from them, but it's still possible. For example, when I was working on my first book, *Visions from Mary*, I often felt the presence of the Blessed Mother. One of the ways that I learned to sense her presence was the fragrance of roses. Even now, at times, Blessed Mother Mary will send me the beautiful fragrance of roses when her energy is around me. So I advise my readers to be open and aware of scents around you. It just may be one of your loved ones or guides trying to communicate with you! Here are some other stories of experiences with scents, beginning with one of my own.

Cherry Pipe Tobacco

When I was small, I'd sit on my dad, Lear's, knee and watch him pack cherry pipe tobacco into his elegant walnut pipe. When he'd light the pipe, the aroma would fill the air. It was a very distinct and comforting smell. He passed away when I was only 14, and for many years I didn't dream of him, nor did I feel he was around me.

Then, when I was in my early 30s, I was going through some major crises in my life and was trying to decide if I should stay with the inner city school district where I taught art. It was very hard to make some of those decisions alone, and I so missed the friendship of my father. One afternoon, I came home from teaching and opened the door to my little condo. In the entrance hall was the unmistakable smell of cherry pipe tobacco!

The smell was so strong and lingering that I knew my dad was there, trying to comfort and help me. The sweet aromatic fragrance was actually there every afternoon when I returned home for almost a week. It made me feel that I wasn't going through this traumatic time alone, and that my dad's love was there with me. Now, every so often when I'm having a rough time, I smell whiffs of his cherry tobacco smoke.

Fragrance of the Caribbean
by Rebecca L.

I just turned 15, and I'm much more aware of angels and departed loved ones around me than ever before. My experiences with the "other side" happen with fragrances. In fact, my favorite aunt, who passed away two years ago, always communicates with me by using an unusual scent.

Near the end of her life, she was suffering from lung cancer and receiving hospice care at her home. Whenever hospice caretakers came, they brought aromatherapy candles and air fresheners for her to use. They said that the fragrances created a peaceful atmosphere for her, and she loved them. I'd visit her every day after school, and we both agreed our favorite scent was "cucumber melon." It was light and smelled somewhat tropical. My aunt would joke with me and tell me it reminded her of her trips to the Caribbean Islands.

After my aunt's funeral, my family went to my grandmother's house to recuperate and get ready to return home. I was sitting on the rug in Grandma's living room when I smelled a faint whiff of cucumber melon. It kind of danced on the air around me. I figured then that someone from my family was burning my aunt's favorite candle, but they weren't. Then, the scent grew stronger and stronger and started to fill the whole house! The strangest part was that the rest of the family didn't smell anything. Only *I* could smell the unmistakable scent of cucumber melon.

Since then, I've smelled the aroma on my birthday and on the day my niece was born. I know it's my aunt's way of communicating with me. She's there for me, remembering our happy times together and letting me know she still sees what's going on in our family.

Grandma's Root Beer
by Mary Ann D.

My happiest times growing up occurred in the rolling hills of Pennsylvania. Summer was my favorite season because that is when our family had many picnic get-togethers. My dad's mother loved to cook, so the food was always excellent. Grandma made everything from scratch, but her specialties were homemade root beer and raisin pie.

Every time we had a picnic, I'd help Grandma spread the red-and-white checkered tablecloth on the picnic table and then, of course, stir the homemade root beer (which to this day remains a secret recipe). I'd savor the wonderful aroma of that delicious concoction every time I stirred it, anxiously awaiting the chance to taste it.

My grandma went to Heaven in 1982, and I prayed for a sign from her. I had read that many times these signs come in dreams and was upset, because often I didn't remember my dreams. Then, about two years after Grandma passed away, I was going through a lot of turmoil in my personal life. It seemed like my life was so bleak that I had nowhere to turn. But what happened next I remember as if it was yesterday.

It was a snowy Friday in January. I came home from work, slightly depressed, knowing I would be spending another night alone. But when I entered my house, I noticed the distinct smell of

Grandma's homemade root beer. It was so strong it almost knocked me over! The smell filled the entire house.

I went from room to room trying to figure out where the smell was coming from, and then it hit me …it was my Grandma's way of saying, "I love you. You're not alone. You'll get through this." My grandmother communicated this to me in a way that made happy memories from my childhood flood my mind. I thought of the many good times we had together, and soon my mood completely shifted. I started to count my blessings and, in the days ahead, felt happier than I had in a very long time.

This was a turning point in my life. Now, whenever I feel down, I just think of the people who loved me. I know that they remember me and love me from the other side. Grandma had a special way of saying hello that comforted me in a time of need.

Scents from the Other Side
by Maureen F.

My sister Mary Jane and I have had many signs that our mother, who died a few years ago, and an aunt, with whom we were very close, are still with us. Sometimes we see a sign. And other times we smell one.

My mother was a smoker, and for a while after Mom died, both Mary Jane and I would periodically smell cigarette smoke. It's not a pleasant smell, but it's very recognizable; and the kind of cigarettes Mom smoked had a distinct odor. So, whenever we smelled them, we knew it was Mom stopping by for a visit.

But the strangest thing of all happened on November 22, a couple of years after my aunt died. On that day, while at work, I smelled Wind Song perfume very strongly, and I couldn't figure out why or where it was coming from. I didn't own any, and a quick check around the office revealed that no one else was wearing it either. Then I realized that the fragrance seemed to be coming from my own wrist!

Thinking I was losing my mind, I asked a coworker to smell my wrist and tell me what she smelled. She confirmed it was Wind Song. Since I knew there was no way Wind Song could have gotten on my wrist, I started wondering …who or what could this be about?

Finally, I remembered that my aunt had worn Wind Song perfume all the time. And today, November 22, was her birthday. She had come to be with me on her very special day!

Chapter Seven

Multiple Sensory Experiences

"Life is real; life is earnest and the grave is not its goal.
Dust thou art to dust returnest was not spoken of the soul." – Henry
Wadsworth Longfellow

There are times when individuals are open to the possibility of experiencing not just one but many sensory events at the same time—seeing, feeling, and smelling scents from departed loved ones. Dreams are also a common part of their encounters. These multiple occurrences closely connect people on the earth-plane with those in the spirit realm. The following true stories are examples of such experiences:

The Comfort of Knowing
by Mike D.

Our daughter Danamarie was a very sweet and special girl. It must be a Daddy's pride, but to me she was the most beautiful young girl in the world. She was also spiritually open to energy around her and believed deeply in psychic phenomena. She was only 18 when she was killed in a horrible car accident.

Several days after Danamarie's funeral, my wife Kathy and I were sitting quietly in our family room. It was about 6 a.m., and we were just holding each other. Kathy started crying, and I was trying to console her when all of a sudden we heard our son Nicholas coming down the steps. Kathy attempted to wipe away her tears because she didn't want to upset Nicholas, who was 15 at the time.

I didn't look directly at Nicholas, but I could see a distinct figure in my peripheral vision. He walked into the kitchen without saying a word. Kathy jumped up and went to the kitchen to ask Nick if he wanted to eat breakfast. But no one was there! She looked throughout the downstairs but saw no sign of Nick. So we both proceeded upstairs to see what was going on.

There was Nick in his bed—fast asleep! He had never come down for breakfast after all. I asked Kathy what she had seen and heard. She also heard loud footsteps and saw a figure dressed in white come down the stairs. She assumed Nick was wearing a white bathrobe. It all happened so fast, I wasn't sure what I saw. I thought I'd seen a gray shadow, since I didn't look directly at the figure.

Kathy and I honestly thought we were going crazy. If it weren't for the fact that we *both* saw and heard the same thing, we would surely have thought it was our imagination. We know now that the figure was Danamarie who came to say good-bye to Nick. They were very close, and her death paralyzed him with grief. Since then, Nick has dreamt of her many times.

In addition, all of us have had numerous *sightings* of Danamarie. Drawings have appeared on her bedroom window, as if they were etched into the glass. Lights have gone on and off and flickered in front of us. The phone has rung, but no one has been on the other end; yet we have *felt* her presence. We've also seen a correlation of repeated numbers that represent her birth date—month and year!

I've kept a journal documenting all the events. But the one sign from Danamarie that we value the most is a photo we took of her empty bedroom. When we had the picture developed, we were surprised to see a figure in her bedroom window! It looked just like our Danamarie, wearing her white graduation gown! We truly believe all of these are ways she has been communicating with us. We will probably never get over her loss, but knowing she's still with us gives us great comfort.

Daddy in Heaven
by Tracey N.

When I first saw my future husband in high school, I knew there was something special about him. We instantly connected and became sweethearts. We married right after my graduation—I was 18 and he was 19. We had two great kids together, and now a beautiful new grandson, 18 months old.

We spent most of our lives together, and were married for 20 years. We had a "fairy tale" love for each other—a very deep love. Then, my husband died tragically on January 16, 2004. He was going through a simple procedure called a bronchoscopy at the hospital, and something terrible happened. He coughed so hard that he blew a vessel in his lung and drowned in his own blood! I was on my way to the hospital when the doctor called me on my cell phone and told me they were doing everything to bring him back.

The night before he passed away, I joined him in our family room, where we had a good chat. The last thing he did was turn off the lights in that room, and we went upstairs to bed. Well, the night after his death, I walked into the family room, and two light bulbs blew out! I immediately felt his presence in the room.

From that time forth, many unusual occurrences began to happen. My daughter and I would feel ice-cold when we talked about him. Then, he started to communicate with scents. I walked into the bathroom and smelled his deodorant. In the morning, I smelled his favorite brand of coffee that no one else in the house drank. And, finally, we smelled his bread machine making fresh bread!

My little grandson was always walking around waving and saying "hi!" to his pappy. Our dog would go from room to room barking in the air. The phone rang numerous times, and no one was on the other end. These multiple happenings led me to *know* my husband was with me because I could feel his presence. But the most remarkable occurrence was a dream that my daughter had one night.

She awoke crying and was lying at the foot of her bed. A moment later, she felt someone patting her shoulder, as if to say, "It's OK to cry. Your daddy is fine." She then slowly got up to see who was patting her shoulder. She walked down the hall and entered his office. Automatically, she stopped at its double-glass doors and opened them. There on the balcony was her Daddy! She told me he had a huge smile on his face and very white teeth. He looked much younger than she remembered. He was wearing a white T-shirt and the brown jacket that she bought him for his last birthday.

He was floating a few feet above the ground, and there were brilliant crystal beams surrounding him. Even though it was only a few seconds, the memory will always stay in my daughter's mind. I believe she actually saw her Daddy in Heaven!

Uncle Louie Gets Our Attention
by S. L.

Many years ago, my husband and I had a great boat that we vacationed on. Once, while touring the Chesapeake, I was awakened by someone literally shaking my foot! I sat straight up in bed and thought it was my daughter, who was six years old at the time. But from across the room, I saw that she was still asleep. My husband woke up and asked me what was wrong, and I told him someone shook my foot. He said he had been sleeping, so it wasn't him and told me I must be dreaming. He encouraged me to go back to sleep, and we both drifted off once again.

Later, he sat up in bed and claimed he heard a man's voice calling his name. He walked out to the deck of the boat from our cabin, but no one was there. We were both restless the remainder of the night.

The next morning, my husband said he continued to hear his name being called and also heard a phone ringing several times. (There were no cell phones back then!). He kept walking around the boat to see who was there, but he found no one.

We traveled on the water for a few more days, and, when we returned home, my husband called his parents. They told him his favorite uncle, Louie, had passed away and was buried on the same day that we had our strange experiences. His parents had been desperately trying to call us to come to the funeral but had no idea how to contact us. We know it was Uncle Louie trying to get our attention by saying, "Get up and call home!"

Divine Connections
by Mary M.

I've had some extraordinary experiences with communications from my departed mother and grandmother. I was very sick one summer and many times during my recovery could *feel* my grandmother watching over me. I not only felt her presence, but I heard her speak to me on three separate occasions. All of these experiences occurred at sunrise, while I was quietly sitting in my backyard. The sun was coming up and filtering through the leaves of the trees when the "divine connections" happened.

Grandmother first gave me a simple message about human mortality, which made me feel more at peace about dying. Another time she told me that she was preparing a pathway for my mother to join her in Heaven—which happened a few months later. And lastly, she told me to visit my mother as soon as possible.

My two siblings and I flew to Florida about four months later, in December, just in time to say good-bye to her. I've always been the closest with my mother and couldn't stop hugging her. I cried the whole way home on the plane and even wrote some special things about my mother in a journal. I felt I was never going to physically see her again—and that turned out to be true. She passed away a couple of weeks later.

We were so close that I knew she would start to communicate from Heaven. She appeared in numerous dreams, comforting me and giving advice. Nothing, though, prepared me for the variety of scents she left in my home! First, the fragrance of Mother's unique cologne wafted throughout the house, then the delicious smell of her infamous chocolate chip cookies baking, and even the scent of her Ponds night cream—which only she used. And, on my son's next birthday, she *appeared* in the kitchen doorway for a couple of seconds—everyone at his party saw her!

I feel so blessed to have had these encounters and always tell others to be aware of promptings from the other side. If you're open to the possibility of communications and patient with your departed loved ones ...you too may experience a "divine connection"!

Pink Roses
by Fred L.

In 1966, I was only a year out of high school. I was a carefree teen, straddling adolescence and manhood. Until then I had never really experienced a mature relationship with the opposite sex, but then I met a girl in my hometown and we fell in love. Betty was the first woman with whom I began to picture myself married and starting a family. However, we were very young—Betty was in her senior year of high school, and I was just 19.

Betty and I began to think about marriage some time in the future, but there was a more immediate problem. When we met, I had just enlisted in the U.S. Air Force, because I had little choice during the Vietnam War years. In fact, the day after I enlisted in the Air Force, my draft notice for the Army was in my mailbox! Although our feelings were intense, just weeks after we met I was off to four years in the military. When we parted, Betty and I were, in a sense, unofficially engaged. I was optimistic that I would not have a short life during wartime, but there was also the reality that guys my age were dying every day in Vietnam. My heart ached at the end of each day—lying on my bunk in basic training and looking at her picture. I so looked forward to the time when I could come home to her.

Though I came home safely from Southeast Asia, Betty and I were torn apart by fate and my own foolishness. Following a brief engagement with a girl I met during my first year in the Air Force, I married for all the wrong reasons. Needless to say, it ended in divorce shortly after my discharge, but I now felt unworthy of Betty and ashamed to contact her. Then, in April of 1971, as I was reading the newspaper, I came across a news story that stunned me into disbelief!

Betty had drowned accidentally while swimming in a private lake in North Carolina. Apparently, she had a seizure of some kind and disappeared beneath the water. By the time rescuers found her, it was too late.

The full impact of that awful twist of fate did not hit me until I went to the funeral home and saw Betty's lifeless body. It was at that very moment when the full weight of the mistakes that caused us to separate fell on me like an asteroid. In that instant, I knew that Betty was the woman to whom I should have stayed loyal and married. The tears flowed as they never had before, and the pain of bitter, hopeless regret engulfed my body. I nearly came apart, as I had never known such anguish.

When I came home after the funeral, I went into the living room of my parents' house (where I was living at the time) and suddenly smelled the scent of roses, although there were no roses to be found in the house, nor did my mother use any kind of floral air freshener! A day later, I found pink rose petals on the floor of the same room! Again, no other flowers were in the house, and there were no pink roses at the funeral. But at the time, I just wrote it off as having some other logical explanation.

For the next six weeks, I sailed a journey of grief and poignant discoveries, getting to know Betty through her family and friends and browbeating myself for being so foolish. Then, one night I crawled into bed, feeling pathetic and at the lowest point I had felt since Betty's funeral. I cried quietly and finally fell asleep. During that night, I experienced one of the most profound experiences of my life ...one that would change me forever!

Some may think that it was a dream, but it was more vivid and memorable than any dream I had ever experienced. First, I had a vision of Betty dressed in a luminescent white gown, surrounded by angels and holding a pink rose. She seemed to be quite peaceful. Then, I found myself floating above my bed, close to the ceiling of my room. Oddly enough, I did not see my own body, but I can still recall every detail of the room and bed—even the wrinkles of the sheets! I did not see any bright light, but I did hear a voice. Though neither female nor male, the voice was compassionate, very clear, and yet very firm in tone—as though telling me what I must do:

"Your grief is well taken, but your place is among the living!" They were the only words spoken, but they were quite clear and audible—at least in *my* head, but the words seemed to be coming from somewhere else. I then found myself back in my bed, falling into a deep sleep, and not remembering anything else that night.

The next morning, I awoke and felt as though a fog had cleared from my head. The weight of the world had been lifted from my shoulders. The message had been heard loud and clear, and I instantly snapped out of my self-pity!

Over the years since then, there have been times when I've smelled roses in the room. However, I have always kept in mind that my day will come soon enough and that, for now, *my* place is "among the living." Betty taught me how to take the love someone has for me and cherish it and not be reckless with that love. We must show those we love how much we care while they are *alive*. Betty will always be a bittersweet memory, but at least I know ...*she* is at peace.

Chapter Eight

Animal and Insect Messengers

"The voice of Nature loudly cries, and many a message from the skies,
That something in us never dies." – Robert Burns

Deceased loved ones are capable of sending us messengers in many forms. When I was compiling stories for this book, I received many fascinating examples of how a spirit can overshadow animals, birds, and insects. Here are stories about a couple of encounters I've had with loved ones sending messengers, followed by others' stories.

Soaring to Heaven

My mother Dorothy and I were more like friends than mother and daughter. She was an intelligent, beautiful, and spiritual being. We are "old souls," and I chose her to be my mother before I incarnated here. Dorothy loved birds—which are "symbols of the soul"—and she had images of different types of birds on porcelain plates, prints, and even pillows.

Dorothy had a somewhat long, lingering passing and was very tired when she finally made the transition. I remember that final phone call as if it were yesterday. It was a Friday afternoon, April

30th, 1993. The nursing home called me to say my mother's breathing was labored and asked me if I could drive up to see her. But before I could hang up the phone, the nurse said, "I'm so sorry; your mother just passed away."

I was stunned that I couldn't be there for my mother. At the time, I lived next to an art gallery that I owned, and a client was supposed to meet me within 15 minutes of the call. I was still in shock as I went over to put a note on the gallery door saying that my mother had just passed away. Suddenly, something told me to open my door, and, when I entered the front room of my gallery, there was a live bird inside sitting on a ledge! It was a small, bright red bird, with a little pointed cap (or tuft) on top of its head and tiny, black, shiny eyes. I had never seen a bird like it before!

I slowly walked over and stood in front of the bird. It cocked its head and looked into my eyes. I automatically extended my hand, and the little bird hopped right onto my palm. Its little heart was beating rapidly against its chest. I walked to the front door, opened it, and let the red bird fly free. But instead of flying horizontally to a nearby tree, it literally shot straight up into the air, and I watched it disappear.

Later I realized the bird was Dorothy's way of saying "Good-bye, Michele. I'm free of pain and worry. I'm free to soar to Heaven undaunted!"

Oscar's Tiger

This next story is, to me, a miraculous one that is very typical of the way a departed loved one can communicate. My husband's father, Oscar, was an intriguing man. He went back to college at the age of 78 to receive his Ph.D. He wrote many books on history and was an avid cat lover. We'd spend many hours talking about the history and breeds of cats.

Oscar was mesmerized by tigers because they are one of the only large cats that like water. Ironically, my husband's nickname is "Tiger Paws" and mine is "Tiger Lily"! A week before Oscar died, I sent him a card. On the front was a regal Bengal tiger swimming in a pool of water. Inside the card I wrote, "Keep your chin up, just like this tiger, and get well!"

Oscar passed away in September 2001. In one of the last pictures taken of him, he was playing with our two beautiful Balinese cats, who are brother and sister. I mourned my father-in-law's passing and was trying to get over the loss. One month later, in October, I was drawn to go outside and look at the moon. It was a sparkling clear night, with stars twinkling. I looked up and said, "Oscar, if you've arrived safely over there and are at peace, please give me a sign."

The next morning, I was standing at the kitchen window, looking out over our hill at the beautiful wooded tree line. Through the trees and down the hill walked a tiger cat with enormous chartreuse green eyes! It proceeded to walk directly to my back kitchen door and sit down in the sun, while it looked in at me. It was an eerie feeling to look into those big tiger cat's eyes.

The cat, which appeared to be about a year old, would not leave our house. If I was up working in my second floor office, it would climb the outside spiral staircase to look in at me. It stayed in the back yard for about a week, going from window to window, staring in. Finally, one night around 3 a.m., I heard crying. It sounded like a baby, and I sat straight up in bed! The temperature had plummeted to about 28 degrees that night, so I went downstairs and turned on the outside light. There was the tiger cat begging to come in and get warm. I grabbed a blanket and went out to hold her. She collapsed in my lap, put her head on my shoulder, and looked lovingly into my eyes.

The next day, I took the cat to the vet. Since she was a stray, we had to leave her at the vet's office for at least a week, just to get her "ready" for the introduction to our other two "indoor" cats. Later, I remembered that, when I was a child, I had a favorite tiger cat I named "Oscar"! Well, what other sign could I need? The funny thing is that this cat hops into the tub and just loves water!

Kristen's Blessing
by Joanne E.

My 27-year-old daughter Kristen died two years ago in a tragic accident. My husband Dan was with her when she fell from a ladder and experienced severe head trauma. Since that moment, Dan has blamed himself for her death—a heavy burden for anyone to carry.

Despite her young age, Kristen made her wishes known about wanting to be an organ donor and to be cremated. She wanted her ashes to be scattered in the ocean, and, when we were strong enough, we followed through with her wishes. We drove to Chincoteague, Virginia—a place she'd always loved and where we had spent many enjoyable times as a family—and scattered her ashes in the Atlantic Ocean there.

The first Thanksgiving after Kristen's death, we traveled to Virginia again to be "near her" for the holiday. On Thanksgiving Day, we went to the beach and tossed handfuls of flowers into the sea. Dan and I stood in silence as we watched our small tribute to Kristen float away on the waves. There was no one in sight—not even a seagull—just my husband and I alone with our pain. All we heard was the roar of the ocean.

We both walked off in different directions, hugging the surf. When my husband and I finally walked back together, he told me an amazing story. He asked me if I had seen what he saw, and I said I hadn't. It seems a seagull had retrieved one of the flowers we had tossed into the water and dropped it directly at my husband's feet! He felt it was as if Kristen was saying, "It's OK, Dad. I'm here with you, and it's going to be alright."

In that moment, we sensed Kristen's love with us on the beach, and we also felt the depth of her blessing. It made Dan realize that she didn't blame him for what had happened, so he could begin to let go of his burden of guilt. We could go on with our lives, even without Kristen's everyday presence, and we knew everything was going to be fine.

A therapist later told us not to "read too much" into the incident. But I'm certain we were seeing the hand of God in that moment on the beach. I will forever believe that Kristen was with us that day and that she visits us often.

My Precious Gift
by Michele B.

Since I was just a little girl, I have loved animals. They give us pure, unconditional love. My mother and father were alcoholics and were very abusive to me, both physically and mentally. Starting at the age of 3, I would turn to my puppy Nootsir for love and comfort. My mother Mary passed away very suddenly on Thanksgiving Day—November 27, 2003. Her death was a shock, and I tried desperately to heal and forgive her for all the years of abuse.

In December, about two weeks after she passed, I started to have visions of a dog's face. I know it sounds odd, but it continued every night for about six weeks. When I was in the shower every evening, this sweet, precious puppy face would appear in front of me. I would wish it well and send it love.

Each night, the little face became clearer. Its long buff-colored fur, black-tipped ears, and sparkling eyes were compelling. I looked up dog breeds on the Internet because I didn't recognize the puppy's breed. I found out it was the face of a Tibetan spaniel. It was a purebred dog and somewhat rare.

One day, my husband Walt took our dog Willow to play a game of fly ball at the local dog training center—there's a large open field behind the facility. Walt happened to run into my friend Kay, who is the head dog trainer. She told him she'd rescued an abused dog and had to pay to get him away from his cruel owner. Kay wanted to breed the dog, which was only 8 months old, but didn't like his personality. In other words, they just didn't get along.

Out of curiosity, the next day, I visited Kay and her newly rescued dog. She walked out holding *my puppy*! It was a Tibetan spaniel—with buff-colored fur, black-tipped ears and a look that could melt any heart. I gasped as I held the softest bundle of love I'd ever seen. He was *mine*! His name was Le Roi, which means king in French, but since I'm hard of hearing, I though Kay said "Leroy." Well, I bought Leroy from Kay, and he's the best dog I've ever had.

It occurred to me that my mother Mary sent me a vision of Leroy and led me to want to adopt him. I feel that Nootsir overshadows Leroy. It was Mary's way of sending a gift to me of unconditional love and forgiveness—something she couldn't do while on the

103

earth-plane. I now have made peace with my tormented past, and it brings me comfort to know that my mother has made peace too, by providing me with a very precious gift.

Dad's Butterfly
by Phyllis B.

Dad was always a big Pittsburgh Steelers fan, and he took me to many of their games when I was growing up. He passed away suddenly in July, 1999. His funeral was very emotional and moving, as many friends and relatives came to pay tribute to him. Before Dad died, I asked him to please communicate with me from the other side, and I knew he would somehow, in a very special way.

The day after the funeral, I went back to the cemetery and stood at Dad's gravesite. A yellow and black swallow-tail butterfly flew back and forth and finally landed right on his grave. As I stared at the butterfly, it dawned on me that yellow and black were the Steelers' colors!

Since then, whenever I'm feeling down or really missing my Dad, a yellow and black swallow-tail will fly by. It's fleeting, and it's like Dad saying, "I'm here for you, but I must be gone." I planted a butterfly bush in my garden in his honor. Now, every summer, I look out my window, and there will be Dad's butterfly in the bush. There's no doubt in my mind it's his way of remembering me.

Note from Michele: The butterfly is a "symbol of the soul." It represents transformation and change. The caterpillar encases itself in its homemade casing (representing the physical body). It is then changed into a beautiful butterfly, to fly free (representing the soul). This is a miraculous transformation. Its hair is changed to scales—a million per square inch; the many legs of the caterpillar become the six of the butterfly; its color changes; and the crawling instinct becomes a flying one. The butterfly personifies the "dancing joy of life."

Watch for the Cardinal
by Ava T.

What a beautiful person my sister was! We were only two years apart in age and were very close emotionally, but she died of leukemia when she was only 28. Her bright light had diminished on Earth, and we sorely missed her.

One night, I had a dream that my sister was standing in a meadow of wildflowers, with a tree line of pine, spruce, and fir trees behind her. In one of the green pine trees was a bright red cardinal. My sister stretched out her hand, and the cardinal flew over and landed on it. As it landed, I heard my sister say to me, "Ava, the cardinal brings good health and vitality." Then she smiled, and the dream ended.

When I awoke, I wondered what the message meant. I realized red was the color of the blood stream, and I had also heard that red was an *energizing* color to wear. I thought that perhaps, since her leukemia was an imbalance of red and white blood cells, she was saying the cardinal was a messenger for my good health.

A few weeks later, on a beautiful day in May, I heard singing outside my living room window. I looked out, and there was a bright red cardinal in our dogwood tree, looking in at me through the window. It gave me chills. I felt as if my sister was saying "hello" through the bird. Then, I realized it was her birthday! So to me, it was not a coincidence that she had chosen that day to visit.

About a month later, as I was driving home from work, a cardinal flew up against my windshield. It startled me, but thankfully, the bird wasn't hurt. Again I knew it was just my sister saying "hi." Now, over the years, the cardinal has become a symbol of my sister's love from the other side. If I'm not feeling well, someone out of the blue will send me a card with a cardinal on the front. And, last year, an acquaintance gave me a cardinal Christmas ornament, without knowing its significance.

It's amazing and wonderful that my dear sister consistently lets me know that she's fine and that she also extends "good health and vitality" to me by sending the bright red cardinal. It's something that makes me feel grateful and loved.

Dragonfly Messenger
by Sherrie L.

My mother was a very special lady. She was from the "old school"—very gracious and loving. She adored nature, gardening, and her family. Many times when she was gardening, a dragonfly would land on her shoulder or fly by, then hover above. The dragonfly became her symbol—kind of a theme for her. She even started collecting them—from pins to lampshades!

She was strong to the very end of her life and passed away peacefully, but the whole family fell apart after she passed. She was the glue that held our family together.

We were gathered outside on the day of my mother's funeral, and the immediate family was seated in front of the casket. As the rabbi started his prayers, a dragonfly came up, stopped, and hovered very close to each one of us in turn. I mean, so close that I could see every detail in its little face!

When we all got back into the car, I asked what everyone else thought about the dragonfly. Everyone saw it and thought the same thing: it was Mom's messenger. We said "thank-you" to her for sending us something that we would recognize. It was a beautiful and comforting sign that she was still with us.

We all live in the Northeast, but she was buried in Florida; so a year later, the family made a trip back down to visit her grave. My sister and I walked up to the grave first and couldn't believe our eyes! Sitting on top of the headstone was a dragonfly ... just waiting for all of us to return!

Grandpop's Deer
by Harold N.

In the winter of 2000, I had a very powerful and moving experience, one that I'll never forget! My Grandpop John and I always went deer hunting together when I was growing up. Now, every time I walk in the woods, I think of him, even though he went to his "happy hunting ground" on the other side several years ago.

On this particular cold winter day, I was deer hunting with my buddies. We heard shooting all around us, and, before we knew it, two doe came running toward us. They stopped a few feet from us and looked directly at me! We knew it was still "bucks only" season, so the doe were safe.

Just then, the strangest thing happened. One doe moved up closer to me and looked right in my eyes, and I distinctly heard my Grandpop John's voice say, "Hi, Harold, it's me!" I just froze in my tracks! I thought I was hearing things. Then, both deer calmly turned around and lay down, so they could watch the other hunters. They remained right in front of me for a long time.

After a few minutes, they both slowly and calmly stood up and turned to face us. I made eye contact again with one of them, and I heard Grandpop's voice whisper, "See ya later!" Then, they both disappeared back into the forest.

It was the most awesome experience of my life. My buddies said they had never seen anything like it in all their years of hunting. Since then, I've only told a handful of people about this encounter. But I know in my soul it was Grandpop John sending me a messenger, in the form of a deer, to let me know he watches over me in the woods.

A Frog in My Path
by Nancy W.

My Grandma was a very intuitive and wise woman. Over the years, as I was growing up, she taught me many wonderful lessons. After a long period of her health going downhill, she finally passed away. I was terribly heartbroken.

The day after she died, I was taking a walk in my neighborhood, feeling very sad and thoughtful. I prayed for her to give me a "sign" that she could hear me and was at peace. Just then, a small frog jumped in my path! I knew it was a sign from Grandma because she and I used to catch frogs at the beach and then later let them go. And, growing up, my daughter collected everything associated with the character "Kermit the Frog."

It was very rare to see a frog in my neighborhood. I knew from experience that they usually congregated at the river or near other water, not on the sidewalk. In all the years of walking that path, it was the first and last time I saw a frog, and I'm convinced it was a messenger from Grandma.

Note from Michele: Indeed, frogs are associated with water, and the water element personifies the "feminine energies." It's a symbol of metamorphosis—going from one stage to another. In the true metaphysical sense, the frog is a "healer of emotions," a cleanser of negativity. It's interesting that Nancy's Grandma would choose to send her a frog—not only because of past memories together but also because of what "frog medicine" personifies.

The Harbinger of Spring
by Robin M.

My lovely grandmother passed away some time ago, and her favorite pastime was bird watching. Towards the end of her life, she'd spend many spring and summer hours sitting on the bench, near the birdbath and feeder. My daughter, who is now 15, vaguely remembers my grandmother; and my son, who is 3, never met her.

It's interesting that my son also loves birds! He draws them, points to them and even chases them. There is one particular bird— a robin—that visits my patio on a regular basis. Believe it or not, for some reason, it stays all year! We've even seen it in the snow, which is quite rare.

My son is particularly fascinated with this robin and one day pointed to it and said, "That's from Gramma." I asked him what he meant and he just shrugged his shoulders and repeated the sentence. That gave me the chills!

I know that the robin is the "harbinger of spring." This correlates to my grandmother being born in April and her favorite holiday being Easter. Additionally, it also dawned on me that my own name is Robin! Could my grandmother be acknowledging my son and me by sending the bird? We tend to think so, and we are so grateful for her communiqué.

Praying Mantis
by Gerald W.

Recently, I was speaking to my daughter about wonderful memories we both had about her mother, my deceased wife. My wife loved butterflies, and, not long after she passed away, I noticed that whenever I'd be walking in nature, lots of butterflies would appear at once and follow me along, some even landing on my shoulder. My wife was an author, and there is a beautiful, bright blue butterfly on the front page of her book. That became our symbol, and that's how my wife communicates with me.

As we talked, my daughter said, "Dad, we have to make a pact like you and Mom did, so you can send me a messenger. You can let me know if indeed there is an afterlife and that you're safe and happy. What about a dragonfly?" I told her I thought that was too common. So she said, "How about a lightning bug?" I laughed and said, "Yes! And I'll land on your nose!"

As I thought about it, though, I decided the lightning bug was also too common. Finally, I thought of a praying mantis! My daughter didn't even know what one was (when was the last time you saw one?), but she agreed.

Two days later, the Philadelphia Eagles were playing their first home game in their new stadium. We watched with anticipation. Suddenly, for no reason, the camera moved off of the action and zoomed in and showed—on national television—a praying mantis sitting on the field! All my kids and millions of others saw it. It was confirmation for me that, believe it or not, when I'm gone, I'll be sending my kids a messenger. And it'll be a praying mantis!

Chapter Nine

Communication through Inanimate Objects

"Nothing in the world is single,
all things by a law divine in one spirit meet and mingle."
– Percy Bysshe Shelley

As I was compiling chapters for this book, I was amazed at the number of stories that were submitted involving spirit communication through inanimate objects! They ran the gamut from baby dolls and bells ringing to car license plates and flying cheese knives! I was enthralled by these stories because they are not the "norm" in terms of seeing, feeling, hearing, smelling, or dreaming about spirits. This chapter provides even more confirmation that you are never alone. The first story is in honor of a special person in my life and how she made her presence known to me after her passing.

An Unspoken Promise

Because I was fragile and rather sickly as a child, my stepsister hired a nanny to help my mother take care of me. Her name was Loretta, and she was a faithful and dedicated person. She had been a "slow learner" in school and by today's standards would be called "mentally challenged."

Nonetheless, Loretta taught me many things—to love and respect animals and humans, to lean on faith, and to retain the "childlike spirit" within me. Most of all, she was funny and quite unassuming. Loretta was a part of my life from the age of one month until she passed away when I was 32 years old.

About a year before Loretta passed away, I awoke one morning and heard a voice say, "Visit Loretta and give her one of your 'Golden Iris' prints." Loretta loved flowers, and one of my most popular prints at that time was a beautiful iris painted against a black background. She lived only a few blocks from the inner city school where I taught art. So, that morning, I put a framed iris print in my car and ended up surprising Loretta over my lunch hour.

Loretta's mother, who had lived with her in a small row home, had died about five years earlier. Loretta was lonely, and the sight of me holding a beautiful gift delighted her. My last words to her that day were, "Enjoy it, Loretta, but if anything happens to you, promise that somehow you'll return it to me!" I said this jokingly, and she just smiled back at me.

A year later, I learned that Loretta had passed away. It was sudden—she had a brain hemorrhage and fell down a flight of steps. I loved her dearly, and, of course, the last thing I thought about was the "Golden Iris" print. About three months later, though, her presence was confirmed. I pulled into my condo complex after work and saw a stranger walking across the parking lot carrying a piece of artwork. As I looked closer, I recognized it—the print was one of mine.

I walked over to the man and saw the writing inscribed on the back of the piece—it was Loretta's iris print! I was dumbfounded and asked him where he got it. He said he had been to an auction at a row home in the city and couldn't resist buying it for his fiancée— who happened to live directly below me!

Well, I met her, and she was delightful. She was a pianist, and she hung the print above her piano. Loretta kept an unspoken promise and made sure I knew she was very much alive in spirit and still loved me. This one incident alone—when I was in my early 30s—

opened my spiritual awareness. Gee, maybe it was possible for a spirit to "move and create" a wonderful confirmation for those left behind on the earth-plane!

The Secret Code
by Nancy H.

In the mid 1980s, I opened up to the existence of our spirit living after physical death and all things pertaining to the spiritual world. A few years later, I began a deeper journey into my own spirituality and enjoyed sharing my beliefs with my entire family. In particular, I felt the need to ask my dad to try to "open up" to a person's spirit living after death.

My father was a gentle-hearted, fun-loving man who survived the first day on Normandy Beach during World War II. So, I bought him a book entitled *Unexplained Mysteries of World War II*, which described war-related psychic and paranormal experiences by people such as Winston Churchill and General George Patton. These two accomplished men were heroes of my father's time, so I believed this would give credibility to these spiritual ideas and dispel any doubts that he might have about what he read.

I was thrilled that my dad read and enjoyed the book. We talked at length about the stories in it and about our beliefs regarding life after death. Since my dad was ill for a long time and in his late 70s when we had our discussions, I asked him to come back to me from the spirit world after his death to let me know that he was alright. He promised he would if he could. So, we devised a "secret code"—a series or pattern of taps and knocks known only to the two of us.

Over the years, we joked about it and practiced "the code" numerous times. After a visit to see my parents, I'd kiss my dad good-bye and whisper, "Don't forget 'the code,' Pop." He spent his last days in the hospital, and several times during those days, he tapped out the code on the back of my hand. The night before my father's memorial service, I collapsed from exhaustion into a deep sleep. For two days I'd been driving in torrential rain to and from the airport, shopping for food, handling numerous in-person visits and telephone calls, and arranging all the last-minute details related to a loved one's passing.

That night, my sister Ginny decided to sleep in my parent's room with my mother. I was sleeping in the second bedroom alone. At approximately 3 a.m., I heard my father's walker loudly rattling against the wall in my parent's room. The walker had been left in a permanent place in that room since my father had gone to the hospital. At first, I thought someone had gotten up to use the bathroom and had bumped into the walker, and was trying to put it back against the wall—a thought I discounted after the walker took on a life of its own and rattled raucously for well over a minute. Then, I heard a loud pounding against the bathroom door.

At first, I thought an inconsiderate person in the next unit had decided to fix something during the middle of the night. Then, I realized that I had heard "the code." I was stunned for a moment—confused—and began to wonder if I had been dreaming. I got out of bed to investigate and stood outside the bedroom door for a few moments. The entire house was completely silent and still. So, I slowly opened the bathroom door and looked around.

Nothing seemed out of place. I leaned over to look into my parent's bedroom, and it looked as though my mother and sister were still sound asleep. I thought no one could have slept through the noise I heard! If my mother and sister had heard the walker rattling against the wall and the pounding on the bathroom door, they certainly would have been on their feet and awake with me! Again, I began to question whether I heard what I *thought* I heard or whether I'd been dreaming—was any of it real? Too exhausted to deal with what I'd just experienced, I went back to bed.

The next morning, I was the last one to get up. I stumbled out of the bedroom and made my way toward the kitchen for a cup of coffee. But, before I could get into the kitchen, my sister walked up to me and blurted out, "Did you hear that racket last night?" Bewildered and sleepy, and suddenly remembering the night before, I shook my head "yes." I asked my sister what she had heard, and she answered me by asking, "Didn't you and Daddy have some sort of a 'code'?" I shook my head "yes" again, and I asked her again what she heard. She didn't answer me. She led me over to our father's walker. My sister proceeded to demonstrate by rattling the walker exactly as I had heard it the night before. My sister then walked over to the bathroom door and pounded out "the code." It had been a total secret between my dad and me, and I was awestruck when she told me what she heard!

I asked her why she hadn't gotten up when she heard the noise. She said that she knew it was Daddy rattling the walker, and, when she didn't see anyone in the room, she knew he'd come back to let us know he was alright.

What has given me such healing comfort is that it was the strong, healthy, young-sounding spirit of my father who pounded out the code on the bathroom door that night, not the 90-pound shadow of a man he was at his death. My dad promised me he'd come back and let me know that he was OK …and he did! He's alive and well in spirit, and I'm very grateful he kept his promise.

A Sign from Ernie
by Gayla S.

My son Ernie was 21 when he was suddenly killed in a car accident in December 2002, just two days before Christmas. His dad, his little sister, and I all had broken hearts because we were such a close-knit family.

Christmas 2003, the first year after his death, was a holiday we dreaded very much. We just didn't know how we were going to get through the holidays, knowing this time of year was Ernie's favorite.

A few days before December 25th that year, something miraculous was brought to my attention. I work part-time at the local hospital and had developed a warm friendship with Vicky, another nurse who worked there. She also taught a course on "death and dying" that semester at our community college. Vicky was correcting term papers when she noticed that one of her students had enclosed with his paper an envelope containing random photographs of headstones from local cemeteries.

One particular photo caught Vicky's eye, because it seemed like the headstone was glowing. When she looked closer at the photo, she saw my last name etched on the stone, and then she saw my son Ernie's name! It was our son's headstone, which we had carefully designed so it would reflect his personality.

On the upper-right corner, we had a sun laser etched into the granite. Ernie had made a drawing of the sun a couple months before his death, and I had kept the drawing. We had it copied directly onto his headstone. In Vicky's photo, the bright sun in the sky was shining right on Ernie's sun! Its radiance appeared like a giant beam of light from Heaven.

Vicky gave us the photo, and we framed it. Although nothing could have made our Christmas without Ernie joyful, we feel the photo was a miraculous sign from Heaven that he's happy and in the light. Many times since that Christmas, we've asked ourselves, "What are the chances that three people—Vicky, her student, and me—would connect like this?" We believe this was more than a coincidence ...it was a divine sign from our beloved Ernie.

I Believe
by Lisa S.

My mother went into a coma and, after a few days of caring for her, I finally told her that it was OK for her to go. The room was dark, and suddenly all the lights in the room began blinking on and off! I felt that this was a message from my mother's soul that she understood what I meant. Later that morning, she passed away. At that moment, my electricity at home went off ...just long enough to make my digital clocks flash her time of death!

After Mom passed, my father moved into my home, and his room was across the hall from my bedroom. A few years later, he became ill and had to be moved to a nursing home. During a visit with him one morning in the nursing home, the nurse came in to bathe him, so I kissed him good-bye and said, "I'll see ya later." Within 30 minutes, I received a call telling me he'd passed away.

In a state of shock, I went into my father's old room to say good-bye. One thing my dad always did was turn his TV on really loud. It was a constant battle in my home. My husband would turn up his TV in the family room, and then Dad would turn up his TV. As I stood in Dad's room, all of a sudden his TV turned on by itself, with the volume really LOUD! I knew Dad was there telling me everything is OK and good-bye! I believe the soul is eternal and find it interesting that both Mom and Dad chose to confirm their existence through electricity!

Baby Doll Messenger
by Sharon J.

Many years ago, my first-born daughter Melany was given a cloth-bodied doll as a birthday gift from my mother. It was from the Madame Alexander Collection and was called "Baby Huggins." However, Melany was a tomboy at that time and never liked dolls.

So, it was no surprise to me when Melany chopped off most of the doll's hair, soiled her clothes, and broke off the edge of her finger. With that, I threw the doll away, but later, my mother pulled the doll out of the trash and said she couldn't part with it. I thought this was odd; however, I didn't question her or try to stop her. My mother then proceeded to place the doll on the top shelf of our bookcase, where it remained for several years.

My first marriage didn't last, and I married my second husband Jimmy when Melany was 7 years old. Jimmy and I had a beautiful little daughter together whom we named Dawn. Dawn was a very special child and loved everyone. From the time Dawn was a baby, she would point up to the top of the bookcase where the cloth doll sat. Finally, one day, Jimmy handed her the old "Baby Huggins." From that day on, it became Dawn's favorite toy, and she re-named the doll "Baby Dawn." The doll went everywhere with her, and she refused to go to sleep without it.

When Dawn was only 4 years old, Jimmy walked out of the marriage. I was devastated with the second divorce and the reality of being left with two young daughters to raise alone. But the survivor that I am kept me going. As Dawn grew older, "Baby Huggins" was once again placed on the top shelf of the old bookcase. By then, I couldn't part with the doll either.

Time marched on, and Melany had a baby girl named Katelyn—my first grandchild! Katelyn looked like a little angel and soon became our family's center of attention. When she was only 18 months old, we received horrible news. My ex-husband Jimmy had committed suicide! The girls hadn't seen him for several years, and he had *never* seen Katelyn.

Two weeks after we learned of Jimmy's death, Melany and Katelyn came to visit. We put Katelyn upstairs to take an afternoon nap and kept the door ajar so we could hear her when she woke up. We were downstairs in the kitchen, talking about life in general, when we heard creaking on the stairs. We ran to the landing, and there was Katelyn crawling backwards down the steps. We gasped when we first saw her because we couldn't believe our eyes—she was dragging the "Baby Dawn" (Huggins) doll down the steps with her!

The doll had been wedged on the top shelf of the high bookcase in the room where Katelyn slept. No one else was in the house except us. There was *no way* the baby doll could have gotten into Katelyn's little hands—unless it had been *placed* there! As Melany and I looked at each other, we could actually *feel* Jimmy's presence! We realized that this was his only daughter's favorite toy. And we knew that, *somehow*, Jimmy handed it to Katelyn to say, "I'm with you, and I see that you're my new granddaughter!"

We also know now that messengers come from the spirit world in many ways. To this day, it still amazes us that Jimmy used a simple baby doll to say "hello" and acknowledge our new baby Katelyn.

Timely Greetings
by Carole B.

Mother was a strong-willed lady and a very special person. We all knew she was a wonderful homemaker, cook, and gardener. She also was the proud owner of an antique-looking clock. Before she passed to the other side, Mother gave me the clock and told me to take good care of it. I put her precious clock on my fireplace mantle where I could enjoy its lovely chimes.

When Mother first passed over, I dreamt about her often. Then, on the first anniversary of her death, something very strange happened with the wind chimes on my back sun deck—they began ringing and making music even though there was no wind! I had chills listening to them and thought about Mother.

A couple years after that, the pendulum on the clock Mother gave me began to stop and start on its own. Time and time again, we'd replace the clock's batteries, but still the clock had a mind of its own. Even now, it sometimes won't move for weeks. Then, if I think about Mother, the pendulum will start to swing. I know that it's her visiting because the clock will start to chime on birthdays, anniversaries, and other special occasions!

Once when my sister Kathy was visiting, I told her my theory about Mother's visits through the clock. At the time I mentioned this, the pendulum wasn't moving. Then, when Kathy was getting ready to leave, I said, "I bet Mother will stop in before you leave." Within a couple of minutes, I looked up and saw the pendulum swinging like crazy! Kathy was amazed!

After that, the pendulum didn't move again until Christmas morning. We were all gathered in the family room to open our gifts. We had the fireplace lit, and everything was very cozy. Then, the clock on the mantle started ticking, and again the pendulum started swinging. It continued until we finished opening all of our gifts, and then it stopped.

It's been wonderful to feel Mother's presence on holidays and special times at our house. I know the ticking of her clock is her way of saying she's with us, and she sees what's happening in our lives. In a way, it makes me feel like we're still together.

Message from the Microwave
by Gayle C.

When I was 21 and in my last year of college, my dad had a heart attack at age 48. Luckily, he survived. My mom called to tell me the news but told me not to come home, because he was out of intensive care and recovering quite nicely. I followed her instructions and went back to studying for exams. A week later, I got a phone call from Mom telling me Dad had had another totally unexpected attack while still in the hospital, and he had passed over.

The shock was overwhelming, but the guilt was even worse. I should have come home the week before to see him in the hospital. I never got a chance to say good-bye or to tell him that I loved him.

The truth was, though, that my dad and I weren't very close. I had been his firstborn, and, according to my mother, "the apple of his eye" when I was a baby. But, when I was 15 months old, my brother was born, and things changed. Now, my dad, who was Italian, had a son. And, in Italian families, the boys were looked on with more favor than the girls.

So, I grew up not really spending much time with my dad. This was not only because he gave more attention to my two brothers, but also because he worked the night shift at his regular job and worked a second job on weekends. I don't really remember feeling loved by him.

Throughout the 25 years after Dad died, I never dreamt of him and didn't think about him that often. But then, after my 16-year marriage and subsequent divorce, I began dating again and exploring my emotional issues related to men. I started looking more closely at my upbringing, my relationship with my dad, and the mixed emotions I had about him that might be affecting current liaisons with men.

During a particularly low period, when I was feeling sad about a recent breakup, I began thinking of Dad a lot. I realized that a wound caused by my perception of lacking love from Dad had been reopened by the man I'd just broken up with, and I was sorting this out in my head. As I sat in the kitchen one day musing about this over lunch, my microwave oven suddenly began flashing "5555." I hadn't touched it nor had either of my children. When I pressed "Clear," it cleared. But then it came back again, flashing over and over "5555."

I unplugged the machine, figuring that would stop whatever malfunction had occurred and reset it. And, for a second, the problem seemed to be fixed. But then, moments later, the fives started flashing again. I wondered what it meant. Being a metaphysical person who believes that our spirits live on after we die, I thought, "Who is trying to send me a message? And what does 5555 mean?" And then it hit me...

My father's birthday was May 5 (5-5). And 1955 was the last day I was "the apple of his eye." The next day, May 6, my brother was born. May 5, 1955 was the last day I must've felt loved by my dad. A very powerful intuitive voice—a *knowing* inside me—had an explanation for this strange occurrence. Dad had heard me struggling with the pain of my breakup and my own self-doubt about being loved. And now, he had come to tell me (in an odd way sure to get my attention!) that he was there for me, he hadn't forgotten his little girl, and he still loved me.

That incident happened about a year ago, and nothing like it has happened since. The microwave is back to normal now, but this one powerful experience brought home for me the fact that our loved ones know when we need them and want to be there to help. Immediately afterwards, I felt a great deal of inner peace and very much loved. And today, I feel a wonderful connection with my dad that I never had when he was alive.

Miraculous Event
by Dawn W.

My stepmother had been ill for a very long time. We knew the inevitable would happen; however, my mother (as I prefer to call her) had wanted us to continue with our lives, paying no mind to her deterioration. As time progressed, so did her illness. It took a lot out of her, and soon my mom was not the same person we had known in the past. During the week that my sisters and I knew might be my mom's last, we each proceeded with our lives in very different ways.

My youngest sister, who was the closest to my mom, was angry but deeply sad. She stayed with her at the assisted living home, day and night—around the clock. But even she needed to rest, so she decided to retreat to a "common area" in the care home and had just fallen asleep. It was about 5:45 a.m.

My other sister, the middle one, insisted on being by mom's bedside—wanting to help her whenever and in whatever way she could. However, she was also unable to stay awake, and, while sharing some of my mom's favorite music playing on the radio, had fallen asleep around 6:00 a.m.

I, on the other hand, had plans to go on a camping trip. It was to be just my husband and me. And, although we pondered changing our plans, we decided to continue living our lives as Mom requested. So, we went on our trip.

When we go on camping trips, we tend to leave the world behind, enjoying a weekend outdoors without a schedule and without any plans—just peacefulness. For some reason, though, that morning, our wind-up alarm clock (which we didn't set) decided to go off. It was very loud and very distracting, quickly waking me up. I attempted to turn it off, but it refused to be silent. I picked the clock up and threw it across our camper, in hopes it would finally subside. Sure enough it did. In fact the clock stopped running at precisely 6:05 a.m.!

Shortly after the alarm clock incident, we heard a knock on our camper door. It was the news we expected to get some time during our weekend trip. My mother had passed away peacefully, in her sleep, at 6:05 a.m. It was almost like she waited for the perfect moment—when all those who loved her the most were peacefully sleeping themselves—and then she had drifted off into the spirit world.

I believe she waited until my sisters fell fast asleep, since they were right there with her. And I believe she wanted me to know, that although I wasn't there near her side, it was OK. She was now alright and at peace.

I have no regrets about that weekend, and I feel blessed to have experienced this "miraculous event" with my mom's spirit. I know she is always near me, and I love her very much!

Ringing Bells
by Bryna M.

I'm only 23 years old, but I've had many divine experiences. I almost died several times during my childhood, but my spirit guide Miguel (Spanish for Michael) would always appear and say, "It's not your time. Go back!" His message would always be accompanied by the ringing of bells or chimes.

One foggy, misty day in Connecticut, I was taking a horseback riding lesson. The horse did a complete flip in the air, and I went smashing to the ground, breaking my fall with my face! When I fell,

I heard distant bells. Luckily, I only broke my nose, and everyone said it was a miracle that it wasn't worse.

After that, I was involved in two major car accidents that almost took my life. Each time, I heard chimes ringing, upon impact. The bells or ringing chimes have now continued with spirits who have crossed over. My best friend's brother Phillip was killed last year, and he communicates by ringing my doorbell! The bell would ring day and night, but no one was there. My dad then removed all the batteries and wires from the wall, so the ringing would stop ...but it didn't.

Soon after, Phillip came to me in a dream and said bells were a symbol for me during this lifetime—a way that the other side communicates with me. The one-year anniversary of his passing fell on a Friday, and his sister Julie (my best friend) called that morning to tell me to listen for bells. Well, all three of my music boxes played by themselves that day, even though they usually have to be wound up. Also, the grandfather clock in the hall, which hasn't worked for 10 years, started chiming. And, of course, my doorbell rang, and no one was there!

I've heard that Spirit communicates in many ways, and I know now that my communications will always come with the ringing of bells!

Love Never Dies
by Carol V.

My original home is near Baltimore, Maryland. My mother and I had many disputes during my childhood and teen years. Finally, when I was 21, she told me to leave and never return. This hurt me to the bone, but I left and I never looked back.

I got married soon after and raised two daughters of my own. About five years ago, my dad, who was very dear to me, passed away. I was his only daughter—the "light of his life," and I felt loved by him unconditionally. After my dad's death, my brother put my mother in a nursing home and left me with the responsibility of cleaning out the old house.

My mother had told me when I left years before that she was going to destroy or burn all my childhood pictures, which, of course, hurt me very much. And, indeed, as I went through the things in my childhood home, I found no photos of me. It seemed they were lost forever!

About a week later, I was visiting a very good friend, who wanted to celebrate my birthday with me. She has an "island" in her kitchen where she had placed some hors d'oeuvres, and on it I noticed that she had two selections that were my dad's favorites—cheddar cheese dip and crabmeat balls. We sat on the floor of her large, comfortable family room, which was open to the kitchen.

All of a sudden, the knife from the cheese dip lifted up into the air and started spiraling toward us! We both screamed and stood up as the knife dropped to the carpet. My friend walked over to the knife, picked it up and laughingly said, "Whoever is throwing this knife better be careful! I don't want cheese dip on my carpet." She washed the knife and put it back in the dip. We resumed talking, enjoying each other's company, laughing and reminiscing about our earlier days.

Then, it happened again! This time, the cheese knife flew up in the air and spun toward us—a distance of about six feet—and landed straight on its edge, with *no* cheese on the carpet this time. I asked my friend, "What do you think this means?" And she said, "I think it's your dad trying to get our attention!" I wondered why he would throw a knife …and then it dawned on me: his favorite game was darts! He and I would spend hours in our basement playing darts together when I was young.

On my next trip to Maryland, I went down to the basement of our old house and stared at the 1950s dart board, still hanging there. Memories of the happy times my dad and I had together flooded my mind, and I started to cry. Just then, I noticed an old cabinet underneath the dart board and opened it. There was a lot of junk in there, but in the back was a large envelope. I blew the dust off of it and opened it.

To my amazement, inside were *all* of my childhood photos! The one on the very top was a picture of Dad holding me when I was a baby. Despite my mother's demands, my father had loved me so much that he had saved all my photos. Now I have these photos and will keep them and treasure them dearly.

It seems Dad, clever man that he was, chose to use a common cheese knife to lead me to the dart board and then to find my old photos. This said to me, deep in my heart, that "love never dies" and that the souls of our loved ones remain very much alive even after death. They continue to care about us and what happens to us. These photos will now be handed down to my grandchildren along with the wonderful story of how my dear, lovable dad led me to them!

Our Family Prankster
by Evelyn D.

Mom and Dad were married for over 60 years. Until the time he was diagnosed with his illness, Dad had been an active 84-year-old commercial artist who was still teaching art classes for senior citizens and children alike.

Dad had mentioned to us that, when he got to Heaven, he would try his best to make contact. My brother said he remembered one of Dad's friends saying that, back when they were friends in school, our dad was a real prankster and liked to play tricks on his classmates. We thought he might communicate from the other side in an unusual way, but nothing prepared us for what was to happen.

The day after Dad's funeral, my brother and I went to sleep over at Mom's house. I have worn a hearing aid for most of my life, and I keep in on my nightstand. That night, I put my hearing aid directly under the bed skirt on my side of the bed, so I could reach it easily in the morning. Before I went to sleep, I made a mental note of exactly where it was.

At about 4 a.m., my brother was shaking me, and I woke up. I could see him beside the night light, and reached under the bed for my hearing aid, but it was gone! I got up and saw Mom standing in the hall with a flashlight, and wondered what they were doing. Just then, my brother yelled in my ear, "Dad is here!" They shouted that they both heard pencils and pens rattling loudly in a cup in Dad's art room.

When they went to investigate and opened his door, the room was in disarray. All his brushes and some of his art books were thrown across the floor! I was tired and confused, but something told me to get down on the floor and look under the metal shelving unit. I was amazed to see my hearing aid under there, stuck against the wall and wrapped around a metal spoke.

My mother and brother noticed that it was hidden directly underneath the cup with the rattling pens! We knew then that Dad was at work. The prankster had moved my hearing aid into his art room and rattled the cup to get our attention. It was a real game of hide-and-seek, and it was just like Dad to communicate in this funny way from the other side!

My Beloved Art
by Susan D.

Within one hour of meeting Art at our church camp in the Adirondacks, I recognized him as my beloved heart and soul mate. With absolute certainty that I wanted to spend the rest of my life with this wonderful and amazing man, and before even holding hands or kissing, I exclaimed, "I love you! Will you marry me?!" We were a couple from that moment on. Although we were never officially married, we had a Native American ceremony in our back yard to join our spirits together for all eternity. Wanting to proclaim my devotion, I even had a license plate made that proudly announced, "LOVU ART."

Our shared spirituality was of vital importance to us, and we would frequently pray together and ask for signs in response to certain requests. At one point, Art was taking coumadin, a blood thinner, for blood clots. Someone told him that he could use ground-up flaxseed instead of the medication. One day as we were driving down a country road, Art mused out loud, "I wonder if it works; I need a sign." Rounding a bend, we received an immediate answer in the form of a huge 3-foot square sign that announced in bold red letters, "IT WORKS!" Needless to say, we were stunned! The *signs* we got weren't usually that obvious!

Miracles became a part of our daily life, and we often shared our stories at night. It is no wonder then that, when Art became ill with cancer, incredible events and synchronicities continued to occur. The night Art passed over, the sky was filled with silent lightning. And, in the wee hours of the morning before his memorial service, the sky was resplendent with one of the largest meteor showers in recent history—originating from the constellation Leo …a very fitting farewell display for my sweetheart, born under that sign!

I told myself that if Art were present in spirit at the interfaith "Celebration of His Life," I would see an orb (a large bubble) on the video we were making. As a neighbor drummed and chanted in Cherokee, the film showed not just one orb, but literally hundreds of little bubbles floating across the screen. The filmmaker was confused, but I was delighted that Art heard my plea and made an appearance.

Eight months later, it was Art's birthday, and it seemed an appropriate time to put his ashes into the sea, as he had requested. Our friend, Donawa, a Cherokee elder, explained to me the Native American tradition of making prayer bundles with ashes. She said there needed to be four women, representing the four directions, and we were to sit in a circle formation. With squares of yellow, blue, red, and white cloth, we made dozens of bundles with Art's ashes, as we fervently prayed out loud for Art's soul. We finished outside under the trees, standing in a circle, holding hands and singing some of Art's favorite songs.

The next day, Donawa and I drove down to Ocean City, New Jersey, where we were to meet Art's brother and children. About a mile from the boat docks, I suddenly noticed the license plate of the car ahead of me. In shock, and barely able to speak, I simply pointed. It read "ART 1313"! Never before and never again since that time have I seen a license plate with Art's name on it. Knowing that the numbers must be significant, I asked Donawa, "What does 13 mean?" She smiled and answered softly, "It's the Native American symbol for the women's prayer circle." My eyes filled with tears as I realized that Art was constantly with me throughout those two difficult days, and nothing had gone unnoticed.

The boat took us three miles out to sea, and, as Art's young sons poured their Daddy's ashes into the Atlantic, seven huge sea rays, about a yard wide, circled our vessel. It was an unusual sight and one that surprised and touched us. Dear sweet Art, who loved ceremony and ritual, was bringing us joy as we honored him …a man who had enriched our lives beyond measure.

Time Stands Still
by Marlene B.

My wonderful father passed away in a nursing home on a rainy winter evening, a couple of hours after my husband and I said good night. We had visited him every evening but had to leave that night when visiting hours were over at 8 p.m. Then, we received the call that he had passed at about 9:40 p.m. The nurse told us that, when she checked my father at 9:30 p.m., he was still alive, but when she returned to give him his medicine at 9:45, he was gone.

Needless to say, it was quite a shock to us. My mother, who has severe schizophrenia, was unaware that her husband had been in a nursing home for the last 13 months. So, the next day, I went to her house to tell her and her caretaker, in a gentle way, what had happened. Immediately, before I could say anything, my mother told me that the clock beside my father's bed was broken. When I went upstairs to check it, I noticed the time had stopped at 9:40 p.m.! It was still plugged in, and the receptacle was working fine.

I guess my father's spirit knew that he'd be passing over after we left and wanted us to know the exact time he passed. In fact, since his passing, the clocks in our house now stop and start on their own. Even our wristwatches (with new batteries) will stop for a couple of hours and then start ticking again.

My father picked a very specific way to communicate with us. Whenever these incidents happen, I know he's popping in to say "hello."

The Little Reindeer
by Heather C.

I own a specialty gift shop in Virginia Beach, Virginia. In October, 2003, we moved to a new and larger location. While unpacking, I discovered some "weeble-wooble" Christmas figurines from the old store. They had a vintage look and reminded me of my mother, who had died a couple of years earlier. My mother loved whimsical gifts, and Christmas was her favorite holiday.

The figurines were battery operated, and, when you turned on the switch, they would bob their heads, light up, and play music. Unfortunately, none of them worked. My assistant and I tried to turn them on, but all of their batteries were dead. So, I packed them in a bag to give to my husband, so he could replace the batteries.

Apparently, though, I forgot to pack one—a little reindeer who never made it into the bag. It was the cutest one of all. Again, I turned on the switch and shook the little reindeer, but nothing happened. I set the reindeer on my desk in the back office and forgot about it. Periodically, I'd clean the desk and dust the "weeble-wooble" reindeer, but it just stood there still and unmoving.

Then, in December, 2003—a week before Christmas—I was in my file cabinet looking for a customer's receipt when I heard music. When I turned around, there was the reindeer, bobbing its head, lighting up, and playing music! I couldn't believe my eyes, since it hadn't been working before.

I felt chills go up and down my body. I felt very clearly that the little reindeer was my mother trying to tell me, "Everything's OK over here and happy holidays!" Well, my skeptical sister wouldn't believe me when I told her the story. She said I had imagined the whole thing. Then, for some reason, I invited my sister to help me out at the shop on the day before Christmas.

It was a frantic day, and we were very busy wrapping gifts for last-minute shoppers. We decided to close early on Christmas Eve to go home and celebrate. We were locking the front door of the store when we heard music coming from my back office. My sister and I ran to see what was going on. There, on my desk, was the little reindeer bobbing its head, flashing its lights, and playing music!

129

My sister's mouth dropped open, and I calmly said, "Mother is saying hello." And my sister said in agreement, "Seeing is believing!" With that, we locked the shop and went home, knowing that our mother was celebrating the Christmas holiday with us that year.

Chapter Ten

Physical Manifestations from Spirit

"What if you slept? And what if, in your sleep, you dreamed? And what if, in your dream, you went to heaven and there plucked a beautiful flower? And what if, when you woke, you had the flower in your hand? Ah, what then?" -- Samuel Taylor Coleridge'

During the course of writing this book, I received several accounts of "physical manifestations" that occurred in people's lives. So, what, you may ask, is a "physical manifestation"? It is an unexplained spiritual phenomenon—the materialization or dematerialization of an object or objects. The concept has to do with *energy*, which constantly surrounds us. The air we breathe is invisible—but we couldn't exist without the oxygen it contains. The human aura is invisible, but Kirilian photography has enabled us to photograph it.

Sometimes objects can *dematerialize* (disappear) and also *manifest* (appear or reappear) in our lives. God is the great "manifester"— He is the author of creation! Angels and departed loved ones can also manifest objects for us, because they are in different realms or dimensions of love and light. I found the following true stories to be fascinating examples of manifestations. First, I'd like to share a heavenly manifestation that happened to me and is chronicled in my first book, *Visions from Mary.*

Madonna of the Towel

One day, in 1993, I was deep in prayer and meditation. Suddenly, there appeared before me a vision of Blessed Mother Mary. She was petite, dressed in white, and heavenly blue light emanated from her. Mary held out her hand to me and requested I do 12 visionary paintings of her divine feminine energy. I was shocked because I'm not Catholic and thought, "Why has she chosen me—I'm not Catholic?" She smiled and telepathically sent back, "Neither am I!" Then I realized she was Jewish, and she was saying in essence that she is Mother of us all!

This initial appearance and communication led me on a five-year journey of faith and obedience, culminating in my first book, *Visions from Mary*, which was finally finished at the end of 1998. During those years, I asked God and Mother Mary for signs and confirmations of her presence and to guide me as to what was divinely ordained. Spiritual phenomena happened around me—I would smell the strong scent of roses throughout my home in the winter months, *sunbows* (prisms of light) would appear in the sky, and my figurines of Mary would be turned in different directions on certain mornings. Then, a remarkable physical manifestation occurred in July 1996.

One afternoon, I washed and neatly folded the towels and placed them on the side of our tub. My husband and I went out to dinner that evening and when we returned and walked into the bathroom we saw the miracle—the very top towel had formed into a perfect image of the Madonna holding the baby Jesus! I walked over and felt the sculpted towel. It appeared rather hard, as if it were spray starched. No one else had been in our home and I knew this miraculous manifestation was sculpted by the hand of God! The photo of this phenomenon is shown in my book, *Visions from Mary*. It is truly the most extraordinary confirmation I have ever seen in my own life.

A Moment in Time
by Edie M.

I have long believed that those we love never truly leave us. While it's true they aren't physically present, the essence of who they are remains in our hearts forever. One particular experience brought that point home with absolute clarity for me.

On October 13, 2000, I turned 42. The last birthday I had celebrated in my husband Michael's company was my 40th, and that was spent in his hospital room a few months prior to his passing. On my 42nd, I asked him for a clear communication—sort of a cosmic birthday card. However, the day came and went with no discernible message from Michael.

"Hmmm…," I thought, "perhaps, time is measured differently on the other side." On October 14th, I was standing in my side yard with my son Adam and a neighbor, woefully eyeing some decidedly dead evergreen trees. My neighbor was a landscaper, so I asked him what he'd charge to remove the trees so they could leap to their next incarnation as mulch.

Before he could answer, a shiny, silver object caught his eye. He pointed to a brown, sparsely needled branch. I followed his finger with my gaze and was astounded to see Michael's L.L. Bean sports watch that I had given him as a gift more than five years earlier. It was hanging perfectly still on that withered branch. Hands shaking and heart tapping out a staccato rhythm, I asked Adam, "Did you put Daddy's watch on the tree?" Eyes wide, Adam responded, "No, I don't know how it got there."

Hearing the theme from "The Twilight Zone" echoing in my ears, I turned the watch over and noted that it wasn't rusted or waterlogged as it would have been, had it hung suspended from the branch for more than two years. That would have been the last time Michael would have been in the yard anywhere near the tree. I had mown the lawn countless times in the past two years and surely would have noticed the watch. Perhaps, I thought, this was my birthday message—a day late perhaps, but clearly meant for me.

As I peered carefully at the timepiece, which lay in my open palm, a startling image appeared. The time at which the watch had ceased its function was 11:42 a.m., which was the same time I observed on the clock in Michael's hospital room the moment he died. Even now, six months after this remarkable experience, I am left with a sense of wonder and comfort. Maybe Michael was trying to tell me that he'll be with me for all time or that time really doesn't matter. Perhaps he was reminding me that time passes so quickly, and we never know when the instant will come for us each to move on, so we need to appreciate each other every day. Or just maybe, he was taking a "moment in time" to stop by and say that I was on his mind as he was on mine when I marked another milestone in my life.

Pearls from Heaven
by Cheryl C.

A few months before my mother died in 2001, she was diagnosed with cancer and told she had only a couple of months to live. So, she mustered all her strength, determined to visit Florida one last time to say good-bye to her nieces and nephews. They had lost their own mother—her sister—just a year before to the same disease, and so we traveled down to see them.

My mother always loved to shop and insisted on visiting the boutiques on the pier at Clearwater Beach one last time. In one store, she found a pair of exquisite pearl earrings and bought them as a gift for me. She joked that she'd like to "borrow them sometime." I treasured them and wore them with pride. In fact, when she passed away just a month later, I wore them to her funeral.

The next Christmas, my husband surprised me with a beautiful pair of amethyst and diamond earrings, which I also loved. Temporarily, the pearl earrings were retired to my jewelry case, placed carefully in the front row of velvet—safe and sound.

On Valentine's Day, I opened my jewelry case, expecting to wear them that evening. But they had disappeared! No one else had been in our house—just my husband, me, and our young son, Andrew, who wasn't big enough to reach the jewelry case. I looked everywhere for my precious earrings. I even checked the vacuum cleaner, but to no avail. The earrings had vanished.

For many nights after that, I missed my mother very much and had trouble sleeping. On some nights, when I couldn't sleep at all, I'd pray and ask my mother to help me find the earrings. It wasn't the earrings themselves I missed, but the love with which they were given. They were the last gift I received from my mother, and they were very dear to me.

A few nights later, I had a vivid dream of my mother. She looked radiant, and in her hand were the pearl earrings! I awoke and couldn't get back to sleep. I put on my robe and went downstairs to make some hot tea. I reached into my robe pocket for a tissue and felt something round and hard instead. I pulled it out, and it was one of the pearl earrings! I had washed and worn that robe more than once since the earrings had disappeared, and I had never seen the earring there before. I took this as a sign from my mother that everything would be alright and that indeed she had placed the earring in my pocket.

The next week was my son Andrew's birthday. He was my mother's first grandson, and she had loved him dearly. I knew she had wanted to be there for his birthday, but now she could only be there in spirit. On the morning of his birthday, while taking a shower, I said, "Mom, it's Andrew's birthday. I know you'll be with us, but can you show us somehow?"

Later, we had family and friends over, and it turned out to be quite a nice party. Suddenly, in the middle of the party, my niece ran up to me and asked, "What's this?" I almost fell over. In her little hand was the other pearl earring! I asked her where she found it, and she pointed and said, "Over there, right in front of the bookcase." I had vacuumed and swept that morning, and there was *no way* that the earring was there then.

We couldn't explain what happened, but my mother could. She brought my earrings back to me in a dream, and then they materialized right after that. It was her way of saying she was there at Andrew's birthday party. I feel she had "borrowed" my earrings and then returned them from the other side!

An Easter Bouquet
by Kate M.

It was my first Easter alone after my husband passed away. I've always loved flowers, so early that morning I stopped on impulse at my local grocery store and went directly to the floral section of the market. In the long case, filled with a sea of red flowers, there was a small, delicate arrangement that caught my eye. In it were three perfect white flowers.

When I got closer to them, my heart started to beat faster, because I realized they were the same three white flowers I had specifically chosen for inside my husband's casket! Without hesitating, I picked them up and brought them to the checkout counter. There wasn't a price tag on the wrapper, and the florist looked confused and asked me where I had found the flowers. When I showed her, she hesitated and then shook her head—she said these flowers had not come from this store!

She then called over to the other florist and asked her if she knew anything about these three white flowers. The woman said she'd never seen or arranged them, nor had she ever seen that specific cellophane wrapping before. When we finally agreed on a price, I paid and left the store, feeling that these flowers were meant to be found by me. They were an Easter gift from my husband ...one that I truly believe he put there just for me!

The Miracle Money
by Brenda R.

A few years ago, I attended one of Michele Livingston's seminars, in which she told the group about a "miracle money prayer." She explained that "thought plus energy equals form," and we can positively manifest things in our lives that are for our highest good. Michele told us we were here on Earth to have abundant life—the more we have, the more we can share with others. We were told to say, "Dear Lord, this week I am experiencing a miracle regarding money." It could come back in the form of a job raise, opportunities, gifts, finding or winning money, or any other significant forms of abundance. Michele emphasized that the most important thing to say after you received *miracle money* was, "Thanks, I deserve it!"

I've always had low self-esteem and never felt worthy in my life. I just didn't believe in asking for anything for myself through prayer, especially not *money*. However, about a year later, my dog was having severe problems walking, and I feared he had cancer or some other deadly disease. But I didn't even have enough money to take him to the veterinarian because I myself was on medical disability, and it was hard to make ends meet. I love my dog more than anything and couldn't stand to see him suffer, so one night I got down on my knees and said the "miracle money prayer." I said it very earnestly and from the heart. The next morning, the vet's office called and said an anonymous friend had offered to pay all of my dog's vet bills! I felt somewhat embarrassed but relieved when they treated my dog, and he recovered from his illness.

Then, a couple days after I said the prayer, my mother was in the local market and, on a whim, bought a $5 scratch-off lottery ticket—something she had never done before in her life! To her surprise, when she scratched off the ticket, the amount said, "$1 million!"

From her winnings, my mother gifted me with a new home and helped me pay off my debts, and I shouted, *"Thanks, I deserve it!"* Now I say the miracle money prayer weekly, and my entire life has changed. I believe in positive thinking and the power of prayer and know God can manifest whatever we need.

Sacred Feathers
by SuAnn O.

Our dad was the center of our family. We all loved him very much and were heart-broken when he passed away on February 12, 2004—only two months after being diagnosed with cancer. I've believed in the afterlife for a long time and knew somehow that Dad would try to send me a symbol after he died.

Dad loved anything to do with flying, and as a kid his hobby was building model airplanes. After serving in World War II, he even applied to aviation school. So, I pondered what kind of *symbol* Dad might send me. Feathers can be "symbols of the soul" and also represent flying—so I asked Dad to send me white feathers. I considered gray or black ones to be a dime a dozen, even though my favorite book on animal totems says that all feathers are a gift. Still, I asked Dad for white feathers because they reminded me of angels' wings.

The next morning, I took a shower and decided what sweater I wanted to wear. As I unfolded my favorite one, a fluffy white feather about two inches long shot up into the air and drifted slowly back down onto my sweater! I was so stunned as I picked up the feather that I just stared at it. My rational mind started to question where it came from, since I have no goose down pillows or comforters in my home. But then, I just looked up to Heaven and said, "Thanks, Dad!"

Dad's funeral was to be held on February 18th, and the preacher asked us if we had a verse or poem to include in the program for the service. We couldn't find anything appropriate for a tribute, because everything we read seemed so somber. Dad had a great sense of humor, and we wanted a poem to reflect his true personality. Time was running out, and I prayed for guidance about what to use.

The next morning, I was walking my dog and happened to notice a card in the distance, lying on the ground. As I approached, I recognized it as a memorial card from a funeral. I hesitated, but something told me to pick it up. As I read it, tears filled my eyes. It was the perfect tribute for Dad! It was written in the first person and said:

Death is nothing at all—I have only slipped away into the next room. Whatever we were to each other, that we are still. Call me by my old familiar name; speak to me in the easy way which you always used. Laugh as we always laughed at the little jokes we enjoyed together.

Play, smile, think of me, pray for me. Let my name be the household word it always was. Let it be spoken without effort. Life means all that it ever meant. It is the same as it ever was: there is absolutely unbroken continuity. Why should I be out of your mind because I am out of your sight? I am but waiting for you, for an interval, somewhere very near, just around the corner. All is well.

Nothing is past: nothing is lost. One brief moment and all will be as before—only better, infinitely happier, and forever we will all be one together with Christ.

I raced over to the preacher with the card, and requested that it be printed with a sketch of a feather next to it. At the service, I explained to everyone how Dad had chosen this poem by sending it to me in a strange way. Everyone thought it was awesome!

At the gravesite, I asked Dad to send me one last white feather. I had visions of a feather floating down from Heaven and landing on his grave—but it just didn't happen. I then went back to my parents' home and went upstairs to my childhood bedroom. There, on my bed was a tiny white feather! I showed it to my sister, and she agreed it was odd, since no one ever used down pillows or comforters in our old house.

The day after the funeral service, I took my young daughter to the video store, and, on our way in, she said, "Look, Mommy! There's a feather!" She picked up a pure white seagull feather, and I put it in my purse. That afternoon, we visited a bookstore, and on the bottom shelf was a bright blue book with a beautiful white feather on its cover. The title of the book was *Sacred Feathers: The Power of One Feather to Change Your Life.* I bought the book and looked up the meaning of seagull feathers. The book said they represent "peace and eternity."

I know Dad sent us the seagull feather as a message that he is at peace and will be with us for eternity. We still frequently find white feathers wherever we go. I've put the collection in Dad's old cigar box, and every time I look at them, I'm reminded that each one is a blessing of love sent down from Heaven.

An Answer to a Prayer
by Susan S.

A miraculous encounter that changed my life happened when I was only 10 years old. My early childhood was not a happy one, because my mother drank all the time and was mean and verbally abusive to me. I tried to be strong and independent as a child, but my sensitive nature always took over. When I turned 8, my grandmother gave me an heirloom gold cross that had been her grandmother's. It had been handed down from generation to generation. She told me to wear it all the time and never lose it, as it was the only piece of antique jewelry in the family.

I was a tomboy and loved to climb trees and run and play in the meadow behind our home. One day, my mother told me to wear my cross because Grandma was coming to dinner that night. She snapped, "Go put it on right now or you'll get a lickin'." I honestly couldn't remember the last time I saw it because jewelry at that age just wasn't important to me.

I locked myself in my room so I could think about where the cross might be. Was it lost outside in the garden or did it fall off the chain somewhere in the house? For the next few hours, I frantically searched, but to no avail. The cross just wasn't there! I was literally crying myself into a state of frenzy when I collapsed on the floor in my closet. My immediate family had never been to church, and I knew nothing about God, Jesus, or angels. All of a sudden, and for the very first time in my life, I started to pray! I simply said, "Please God, if you're there and you can hear me, bring me the cross."

An unbelievable peace came over me, and I then heard a deep male voice say, "Turn around." When I turned to look at my bed, I saw a shiny gold object on top of my pillow. It was the cross! The cross had not been there a few minutes prior, so I knew God must have sent an angel to bring it back to me.

That physical manifestation changed the whole course of my life. It was a turning point for me to be strong, lean on my faith, and stay in my prayer time. Life has never been easy for me, but when I struggle—I pray. God did hear a child's heartfelt prayer that day and sent an angel to the rescue!

Spiritual Lost and Found
By Nance T.

My mother died a few years ago, and since then she has come to our assistance many times by bringing objects we have lost back to us. She loved her family so much, and anything pertaining to family that's missing is somehow returned—we believe it's with her help!

These "lost and found" experiences began happening about a month after my mother passed. When my son David had his first music recital, my husband Bob couldn't find the video camera charger. So, that morning we searched his den, where it's usually kept, and eventually the entire house. The recital was just a couple hours away, and I said, "Mom, I know you can help. Please show us where the charger is."

A few minutes later, my husband yelled, "Nance! I found it!" Well, I ran into his den, and on top of his desk was the camera charger. Of course, he'd already checked there before, and it wasn't there. I told him my mother put it there. He had a hard time believing me and was a skeptic for a while. But, as time went on, he became a firm believer too, especially after another incident...

My son David became a really good basketball player. The main requirement for basketball registration was to submit a copy of his birth certificate. Bob had taken the original to work to make a copy. The next day, he couldn't find the original or the copy. Time was of the essence, and we had just 24 hours to produce the copy. My son was planning on a scholarship, and he would've been crushed if he couldn't play ball.

We searched Bob's briefcase, coats, and pockets with no luck. We then searched his den and both our cars. We looked under the car's floor mats, between the seats, in the console, under the seats—absolutely everywhere! Then, I told Bob we should ask my mom to help. He said that was nonsense—he wasn't going to do it. He resumed searching and was out in the garage, still looking around, for almost an hour. Finally, he walked in from the car looking subdued and awestruck.

In his hand were David's original birth certificate and the copy. When I asked where he found them, he said he'd been sitting in the driver's seat, very frustrated, and he finally asked my mom to help. About a minute later, on an impulse, he reached under the driver's seat (for the umpteenth time!), and there they were! He then said he had no choice but to believe that my mother had helped him.

Just for Fun
by Jon S.

My mother, Geraldine, was a special lady—one of 11 children who grew up in what is now the Great Smoky Mountains National Park in Tennessee. When she was young, she was a tomboy who loved nature and adventure. She was only 18 when she married my dad Oscar, who was a lieutenant in the Army and stationed nearby. Jerry, as she liked to be called, always loved flowers. She planted all kinds around our house and out in our huge backyard, and I remember her having African violets, patiently tending to them and many times being frustrated while trying to grow them.

Mom passed away in August 2000, and my wife and I inherited one of her fragile purple violet plants. We added this to several other varieties—all of varying colors from white to magenta—that we were already struggling with ourselves. They were all fickle plants and ones that never seemed to flourish. Then, shortly after Mom passed, we noticed that without any change in the way we were caring for the violets, they started to grow profusely. In fact, the purple violets we inherited from her were so large they encompassed about one-third of the coffee table they were on!

Then, one night my wife had a dream of my mother, Jerry. She looked well and very happy and visited my wife for some time in her dream. When she started to leave, she smiled and with her Southern drawl said, "And I make the violets grow, just for fun!" My wife thought it was remarkable that Jerry was tending the violets—from the other side—and that she received such pleasure in doing so.

Many times we feel her *presence* in the room where the violets bloom. We feel this is a perfect example of a spirit or soul being able to manifest love from Heaven to Earth in such a tangible form.

Pennies from Heaven
by Heather W.

A few days after I returned home from my mother's funeral, I was awakened and startled when I sensed something in my bedroom in the middle of the night. At about 4 a.m., I sat up in bed and looked over toward my husband. But, instead of him being there, my deceased mother was lying next to me! I blinked my eyes, but every time I opened them, she was still there. Strangest of all, emanating from her head was a glowing yellow-red light. The light was very bright, like a bright new copper penny. At that instant, I had a strong *knowing* or *feeling* that my mother would start communicating with me by sending me pennies.

Eventually, I fell back to sleep, but the weird apparition stayed in my mind. A few nights later, I pulled down my quilted comforter to crawl into bed, and there on my pillowcase was a shiny new penny! I asked my husband about it, and he just laughed and said he knew nothing about it. From that day on, my mother literally started to throw change at my feet! Every day I found change, in every kind of place—beside my car door, under my bookcase, on the kitchen counter, on floors at malls and restaurants. It was totally amazing!

Frequently, I found dimes and quarters too, but pennies were appearing constantly. One time, while on vacation, I actually heard and saw coins falling from the sky and landing on the pavement in front of me. This morning, I found five pennies and a dime. I've tried to figure out why my mother would connect with me in this strange way, and now I think I have the answer!

She was just a child when America went through the Great Depression. Her family didn't have a lot of money in the early years, and I feel that she doesn't want me to ever go through what she experienced. And so, this is her way—from Heaven—of helping me feel materially secure while I'm still here on the earth-plane.

Nugget's Tennis Ball
by Sandi R.

I'd like to share a heartwarming story about a spiritual manifestation. My husband passed away a year and a half ago, very suddenly at the age of 50. At the time of his passing, our family had a disabled Jack Russell Terrier named Nugget. She was born with only one front leg. Our son saved her by adopting her before she was sent to the pound. Nugget quickly became my husband's baby. She had a fetish for tennis balls, and her favorite pastime was running like the wind, chasing them. She would follow my husband all over the yard and house, pestering him to play ball. Nugget was the only one home with my husband when he passed away of a heart attack. Since there was a tennis ball lying next to his body, we figured he and our little dog had been playing. Appropriately, we included her picture and favorite tennis ball in the vault with his ashes.

After my husband passed, Nugget quickly became my baby and my salvation. She kissed me when I would cry myself to sleep at night, and she was there when I came home from work. She was my companion and snuggle partner at night. On May 25th, 2004 I came home from work to find our back yard gate open and a brand new tennis ball smack in the middle of our driveway! I shut the gate, took the ball in the house, and let Nugget out. I then double-checked the yard but found nothing unusual. I spoke to my son and his girlfriend, and they both assured me that the gate was shut with no ball in the driveway only two hours before I arrived home.

On Wednesday evening, May 27th, Nugget began vomiting and was unable to urinate. Our vet was away, so we were instructed to take her to an emergency center in another town. They kept her several days, catheterized her, and did x-rays and an ultrasound but found no blockages. We brought her home Friday evening, and she did well through Saturday afternoon—then everything started all over again. Our vet said that Nugget must have a major problem that did not show up on the ultrasound.

Facing additional tests to determine what would probably be a terminal problem anyway, we finally made the decision to let her go and end her suffering. The vet needed my son to hold the dog as he gave her the injection because it was after hours, and no one else was there. She passed seconds later in my son's arms and, I'm sure, right into my husband's! We seriously believe that my husband brought back the ball for Nugget to tell us it was alright to let her go. We feel his presence around us a lot, and it's a comfort to know they are back together again.

Celestial Intervention
by Edie W. M.

As a social worker in an acute care psychiatric hospital, I serve patients who are in crisis and in need of immediate treatment. Although I love offering counseling, 80% of my job is case management. This means I help people maneuver through a vast bureaucratic maze to find housing, treatment once they leave the hospital, medication, and the means to pay for all of it.

One Thursday night, I received a call at home from the charge nurse at work. One of my patients was getting ready to leave, but they couldn't find the envelope that had her cell phone, money, ID, and insurance card in it. We always lock valuables up in a file cabinet drawer, and only the charge nurse has the key. A few days earlier, I had borrowed the key to take her cell phone out so she could retrieve some phone numbers from it. I *always* put the envelopes back in the drawer after getting out what the patient needs.

This time, I clearly remembered taking it out of the drawer, but I had no conscious memory of putting it back in, so I began second-guessing myself. The night staff looked through the drawer several times, looked in my office where we had last seen the envelope, and looked in the nurses' station. But there was still no trace of the envelope. I decided to have a brief but impassioned conversation with the angels, asking for their assistance in finding the envelope with its contents intact.

The next morning, I looked in the drawer, took everything out, and checked my office and the nurses' station again, but still there was no envelope. I gazed heavenward and said, "OK, guys, a little help here." A few hours later, I went into my office to do a family therapy session. The day charge nurse approached my door and waved the envelope at the window. I let out a "Yahoo!" in the midst of this intense session and then explained to the family the reason for my outburst.

When we were finished, I asked Katie where she had found the envelope. Her answer? "In the drawer." It had suddenly appeared there when it hadn't been there earlier. I knew without a doubt there had been some celestial intervention …and I was very grateful!

Miraculous Return
by Rosemary R.

A few months before my husband died, he bought me a lovely pair of diamond earrings. They were very precious to me, not only because of how beautiful they were but because they were one of the last gifts I received from him.

On the day we traveled to make his funeral arrangements, I wore the earrings with pride. My daughter had just cleaned them for me, and I made sure both earrings were securely fastened to my earlobes. At the funeral parlor, I needed to make a quick call and removed my right earring to make it easier to talk. Then, I returned to the funeral director's office to discuss some more details.

A couple of hours later, when I was returning home with my daughter and son-in-law, I realized that I had forgotten to pick up the priceless diamond earring from where I had laid it down at the funeral parlor. My son-in-law suggested I call immediately when we returned to see if they'd found it.

The minute we got home, I ran to the phone in my kitchen to call the funeral home and was amazed to see something lying right there by the phone ...it was my diamond earring! We were all in complete shock! Both of them had seen me remove the earring in another town, just a few hours before, and now here it was!

The three of us cried and hugged each other, knowing in our hearts that my husband is the only one who could have brought his beautiful gift back to me. I felt so comforted knowing he was still near me, watching over and helping me.

The Green Fields of Heaven
by Mary C.

My husband, Bud, died in April 1992, leaving my ten-year-old son, Andrew, and me in deep grief. Andrew bottled up his emotions at this tremendous loss. I, on the other hand, could not stop crying at the most unexpected times, but was given God's grace to go on.

There was a local class for travel agents and I encouraged myself to enroll. On a Friday afternoon, in early June of that same year, I arrived home early from my class. It was just my son and me living in the house, and I looked forward to spending quality time with him that day. Andrew came home from school shortly thereafter and he seemed unusually sad. I asked him what was the matter and he simply stated, "I do not want to be here. I want to be in Heaven with

Dad, the cats and you; and we can play in the green fields." I told him that it wasn't our time and that we still had work to do here. Then I suggested that we go see a comedy movie to cheer him up. My son asked if his best friend, Jimmy, could come along, and I said, "Sure—why don't you call him?"

Well, Jimmy's phone was busy so I told Andrew that it would be a lot quicker if he just walked up the street to Jimmy's house to ask him. We seldom use the front door, even our mailbox is back near the garage. But for some reason, Andrew ran to the front door and opened it to leave. A bright stream of light shone strongly on the foyer mat, and there—glistening in the sunlight—was a small cross! This was very unusual, since I am maniacal about keeping a clean home and had just vacuumed that morning. No one had come through that door in a very long time, so how could this unusual cross be there?

Amazingly, Andrew picked it up and said, "This is for me and it's from Dad!" He turned it over and on the back was the first part of the twenty-third Psalm, "The Lord is my shepherd I shall not want, he maketh me to lie down in green pastures..."

Andrew looked at me and said, "Daddy is okay, he's in the green fields now, but we're supposed to stay here."

From that day on Andrew was a much happier child, for his healing had begun. I know in my heart that Bud placed that cross there for Andrew, because of the pain in his little heart, and I also know that when it is our time to go, we'll meet Bud in the green fields of Heaven.

Afterword

At some point in your life, you have been contacted by your angels and departed loved ones. How can you maximize these types of communications?

- **Ask.** Remember to *ask* for them to come to you and be open to *receive* promptings from them. Ask for a *seeing, hearing,* or *feeling* experience to occur.
- **Be Aware.** *Awareness* is the key! So be open to unusual occurrences with appliances, clocks, phones, and radios and to all the different forms of communication mentioned in this book.
- **Think of Them.** When you *think* of those you want to hear from, it will pull their energy around you so they can contact you in a greater way.
- **Desire.** Intense *desire* or *emotions* on your part can trigger a communiqué from them.
- **Pray.** There is tremendous power in *prayer*. It is an emotional *reaching out* to God, the Creator, and also to your angels and loved ones in Heaven.
- **Journal.** Keep an ongoing *journal* and write down unusual or miraculous encounters or dreams.
- **Believe.** *Know* in your heart that they do exist, they love you, and they are waiting to help you.

- **Create.** You might want to create a *special place* in your home to commune with them. A simple stand or end table can be used as an altar. Cover it with a white cloth. Put pictures of angels and deceased loved ones there. Burn white candles—they attract the higher realms to you. Place fresh flowers on your altar. Buy a tabletop fountain for the room—the energy of running water also attracts their energy. Hang a crystal sun-catcher in your window to create rainbow sparkles. (Many times, angels appear as *sparkles*, and seeing them in your room will attract them to you.)
- **Meditate.** This practice stills the mind and gives you a sense of inner peace. Simply close your eyes and take a few deep breaths. *Visualize* in your mind the loved one or angel with whom you want to communicate. Then, be open to *sensing* that entity, and their *presence* will surround you.
- **Be Patient.** Their timing or ways are not always in sync with yours. If you sincerely want them to communicate, let them choose the vehicle through which they'll do that. Let it be in *their time* and *their way*. You will eventually succeed.
- **Be Thankful.** Spirits and angels appreciate your "attitude of gratitude." It's a positive way of *acknowledging* their presence. When you *thank* them, they tend to extend more confirmations your way.

Through all these encounters, please remember that God is the ultimate source. Angels are your messengers and protectors. Departed loved ones are your guides, helpers, and friends. And you are *never alone*.

About the Author

Michele A. Livingston is an internationally known visionary and gifted artist. With a master's degree in art education, she taught art in the public schools and ran her own art gallery. Her own paintings and collector's plates are in demand throughout the world. Clairvoyant from an early age, she has the incredible ability to see and communicate with angels and deceased loved ones.

In 1993, Mary, the Blessed Mother, appeared to Livingston—which astounded the author because she was not raised Catholic! Mary entreated her to paint 12 different images of Mary's divine feminine energy. This event (that changed the author's life) is chronicled in her first book, *Visions from Mary*. A similar spiritual and artistic encounter with Red Cloud, the departed chief of the Lakota Sioux Indians, became the subject of her second book, *Echoes in the Wind*. She has touched thousands of people—one-on-one and in seminars—with messages and actual visions of their departed loved ones.

As a regular television guest of Philadelphia's "It's Your Call with Lynn Doyle" and in other TV and radio appearances, she has astounded both skeptics and believers, and she has been consulted on the subject by film producers. As a healer, counselor, columnist, lecturer, and ordained minister, she continues to bring messages and soul-healing stories to people all over the world and assists people to take the "next step" in consciousness to become closer to the Creator.

Michele does seminars and one-on-one phone consultations. For information please visit her website at: http://www.michelelivingston.com. or call (717)737-3888.